Giles & R,
with love
from
Mother & Dad

June 2000

THE ART OF LEARNING

By the same author

Reginald Fairlie, Scottish Architect 1959

Living in Towns (BBC) 1966

York: City Buildings 1971

Landscape of Ideas 1972

Spirit of the Age (*A Full Life and an Honest Place*)
(BBC) 1975

Leeds Old and New 1976

Leeds 1979

Pocket Guide to World Architecture (*Mitchell Beazley*) 1980

World's Great Architecture (*Editor*) 1980

Shell Guide to English Villages (*Yorkshire*) 1980

The Story of Architecture 1983, 2nd ed. 1997

Mackintosh and his Contemporaries (*General Editor*) 1988

Understanding Modern Architecture 1988

The Home Front: Housing the People 1989

THE ART
OF LEARNING

A Personal Journey

Patrick Nuttgens

Patrick Nuttgens

The Book Guild Ltd
Sussex, England

The Book Guild Ltd.
25 High Street,
Lewes, Sussex

First published 2000
© Patrick Nuttgens, 2000

Set in Times
Typesetting by
SetSystems Ltd, Saffron Walden, Essex

Printed in Great Britain by
Antony Rowe Ltd, Chippenham, Wiltshire

A catalogue record for this book is
available from the British Library

ISBN 1 85776 463 3

CONTENTS

INTRODUCTION

This is part of an autobiography; that is, it is a selection of the many episodes and experiences in what I might, with some arrogance, describe as my career. Its title indicates what most of that career has been concerned with – art and learning. Its three main chapters are based upon the main places in which most, not all, of the experiences took place. The places were the cities of Edinburgh, York and Leeds, in which I have played a part – and usually an influential part – in periods of innovation in education. They were events which, I believe, might (as the Duke of Wellington said of his presence at Waterloo) have been different if I had not been there.

Those three cities are introduced by an opening chapter detailing what I now recognise, as I look back on it, as an unusual upbringing. There cannot be many people who have grown up in a stained-glass studio – and also, I hope, not many people who have suffered the same disasters.

There were two in particular. During my first term as a boarder at prep. school, my mother died. Even with wonderful care and help, this effectively meant that from the age of seven I learned to look after myself. A few years later, again at boarding school, I was struck down by a severe attack of poliomyelitis and spent nearly two years in a hospital, slowly – and never wholly – recovering the use of my paralysed limbs. My story is that of a boy and man in a constant battle to live a normal life. Normal? But then, what is normal?

Partly as a result of that disability, and more because of my upbringing, I have spent many hours drawing and painting as well as reading and writing. The illustrations that accompany these memoirs are taken from some of the many sketchbooks I have always taken with me on my travels. I was trained as an architect and have always drawn places and buildings, so the sketches are comments on people and places I have encountered.

And despite my disabilities, which have recently become worse, I have been lucky enough to travel to many countries in Europe and many other parts of the world, always writing and drawing and lecturing – and, for about twenty years, broadcasting. I hope it makes an interesting story. In particular, in however small a way, it might perhaps give a message of hope to people just as disadvantaged – but able, I hope and wish, to experience the happiness I have always known.

Dad c 1950

1

The Stained-Glass Studio

I was born beneath Whiteleaf Cross on 2 March 1930. Whiteleaf Cross is not an ancient monument: it was cut into the chalk of the Chiltern Hills in the seventeenth century shortly after the Civil War, as a gesture of peace and stability. In my childhood I got to know it well and explored the Cross from top to bottom. It is wider at its base than at the top.

The house was a very ordinary one, but in the garden was my father's studio in which he designed and made stained-glass windows. On marrying my mother, he had rented some rooms in a farmhouse at Cobblers Hill nearby, then moved to Whiteleaf. From there he moved to North Dean and finally to Pigotts Hill.

My father was a quite exceptional character. He died at the age of ninety, having driven himself to hospital, leaving a half-completed window in the studio. It was later finished by my brother Joe and is now in Addis Ababa. Shortly before he died, I gave a lecture about him at the Art Workers' Guild in London entitled (at my father's suggestion) 'Seventy years' work'. He had spent that time designing, making and fixing stained-glass windows. I often watched him at work, and sometimes helped him to cut glass or fix a window. In preparing this book, I stupidly thought that I would find, among his letters and files, information about his life and work. There were no letters, no files, no account boks, no copies of letters, no documents, no cheque stubbs. He may have destroyed them; more likely, he just never had them. There was, in short, no record whatever of his remarkable life, interrupted by epi-

1

sodes of fun, success and disaster. He designed and made at least 300 windows, mostly in English parish churches. Some of the biggest and best were the windows in Hong Kong Cathedral and the great East Window in St Etheldreda's, Ely Place, London.

My father was German, born in Aachen in 1892. His father was an itinerant tailor or tailor's cutter who had travelled in many countries, including England. There he met his wife who was herself the daughter of a tailor in Cambridge. Family tradition has it that as a result of becoming a Roman Catholic, the Cambridge tailor lost all his clients and was, for a time, in the workhouse as a bankrupt. On the other side my German grandfather was a little man who wanted to be a scientist and had the intellectual ability but no means of becoming one at that time. An ancestor in the German army had committed some heinous crime and had been cashiered. The German veil of secrecy was as opaque as that of the English workhouse. I never discovered what he had done. Having lived in both Germany and England, my grandfather finally settled in England. The family lived for a time in Cricklewood and then Harrow on the Hill from which my grandfather took a train to his work in Savile Row every day.

Dad left elementary school at the age of fourteen. It was the only schooling he ever had. It left him with clear speech, an excellent vocabulary and an English accent which sometimes led people to believe that he had been to university. As a working boy, his first job was in a sandblast factory making lettered glass for pubs and factories. Then he got an office job, addressing envelopes and doing some typing.

It was a meeting between his father and Arthur Anselm Orr which changed my father's life. Orr was an artist who designed stained-glass windows for commercial firms to translate into glass. Meantime, my father had started drawing railway engines from the rear window of the house. He was at first entirely self-taught. In Orr's office he was encouraged to apply watercolour to the sketches. But he wanted more than that, so he went to evening classes at

Harrow School of Art where he discovered a gift for portraiture and drawing. I was familiar from the early years of my life with his ability to draw figures unhesitantly on a large scale and never ceased to admire the skill and certainty with which he drew. From time to time he interrupted his work of drawing and making glass to play the piano. The first piano I remember was a very ordinary machine; then he bought a Blüthner and played Bach, Mozart and Beethoven from the early hours of the morning at considerable speed. In the evenings he played folk songs for us to sing.

In 1914, at the age of 22, being a German, he reported to the police station and to his surprise was arrested, handcuffed and driven in an open bus through the streets of London so that passers-by could throw stones at him and his companions. His younger brothers, who had been born in England, were recruited into the English army. His father, on the other hand, who was wholly German, was left free. After a few weeks in a waterlogged camp at Frimley my father was taken to a camp at Stobbs near Hawick in Scotland where he spent the first year of the war.

Having left Aachen when he was three, he could not speak German and was, therefore, unable to communicate with most of the other prisoners who naturally insisted on speaking German. What he did instead was to make drawings of them – portraits, I understand, for which he charged threepence in black and white and sixpence in colour. He said he had an order list as long as his arm when he was released, to the great irritation of the rest of his fellow prisoners. I know there are houses in Germany that still have his drawings. For himself, he seems to have been cheerfully indifferent to what happened. When an American ambassador came to the camp and asked him what he was doing there if he could not even speak German, he simply shrugged and said, 'That's the way it is.' When after a year he was released, he volunteered for the British army and was turned down on the reasonable grounds that he was a German.

Before the war, he had studied stained glass in the Central Schools in London and then worked for Karl Parsons, the Head of Stained Glass in the Schools. Parsons was an exquisite and brilliant artist, whose work derived directly from the Pre-Raphelites: I have no doubt that Parson's work influenced all my father's early drawings. On his release from the camp, he worked for Martin Travers who was later to be Head of Stained Glass at the Royal College of Art.

At the end of the war my father was encouraged to apply for, and was appointed to, that very job: Head of Stained Glass at the Royal College of Art. He loved it. But his employment came to a sudden and rather disgraceful end. He was summoned to his office by Hubert Wellington, the Registrar of the College, who explained that the British Legion had complained about the employment of a German at a Royal College in those post-war years. He asked my father to resign and my father did so without hesitation or protest. Wellington went on to become Principal of Edinburgh College of Art, and that later had an effect upon my own story.

My father started his own stained-glass work with a small window for the Roman Catholic church in Harrow. He then made drawings for the stained glass firm of Whitefriars. He sometimes finished windows for other artists, having earlier discovered a gift for designing in other people's styles. One artist in particular remarked that my father could design his windows better than he could himself.

The other main influence on his career was an organisation in Fulham in London, originally called the Glass House, set up by a Miss Lowndes and a Mr Drury and later, after the Great War when the phrase 'glass house' had a sinister meaning, renamed Lowndes & Drury. It consisted of five studios with associated cutting and glazing and other assistants, enabling an artist to obtain a commission, hire a studio, work out a design, select and paint the glass and supervise the whole operation. Among the artists who used the facilities were Karl Parsons (who had taught him at the

Central School), Martin Travers (whose assistant he became), Wilhemina Geddes (whom he considered the outstanding artist of them all), and Henry Holiday (whose work he later carried out himself).

The book that profoundly influenced him was Christopher Whall's *Stained Glass Work*, edited by W.R. Lethaby and first published in 1905. Its effect on him was profound; for Whall insisted on the importance of glass for its own sake. In his view, it was essential to handle the glass itself and not merely design for it. Such a view was in direct conflict with the powerful tradition which had been built up with the revival of stained glass in the nineteenth century. In the more fashionable cases, it had become the practice – then as again now – for a celebrated artist to make designs for stained glass which were then carried out by skilled but uncreative craftsmen.

But most of the work was both designed and made by a number of great firms which produced a vast number of stained-glass windows during the prolific church-building era of the nineteenth century. Their heyday was between 1850 and 1900 – firms often started by an artist but quickly geared to a system of mass production based upon the division of labour. Clayton & Bell's were at one time said to turn out a window a day and two on Sundays; Hardmans of Birmingham, started by Pugin, was perhaps the greatest; Kempe's the most celebrated. In contrast to these great businesses, my father belonged to the small community who believed in the unity of the artist and craftsman.

Leaving the Glass House one day, he was called back and asked if he would like to take a job in Chipping Campden in Gloucestershire, painting windows for a stained-glass artist, Paul Woodroffe. It was a turning point in his life.

He was free, competent and very skilful, and he behaved in a manner that I later found was characteristic of him. He simply followed where the wind blew him. He was in his early thirties and unmarried. He had taken girls out but never found one to take him in hand. He told me that only once had he thought of proposing to a girl but then, as he was actually pressing the doorbell to take her out, he remembered that she had admired some sentimental repository art that she had seen in a shop window and, appalled by the thought of living with someone of such embarrassingly bad taste, he ran away and never saw her again.

It was quite different when he got to Chipping Campden. He discovered – and never forgot – the beauty of a Cotswold town. He was overwhelmed by its clarity and materials as well as its form and its activities. In particular he became infused with the ideals of the Arts and Crafts Movement. He told me that one of the best statements of its principles was in C.R. Ashbee's book *Craftsmanship in Competitive Industry* (Essex House, Campden, Glos., 1904). Ashbee aimed to translate the theories of John Ruskin and William Morris into a practical reality appropriate for the twentieth century. He explained that

> this Arts and Crafts Movement, which began with the earnestness of the Pre-Raphelite painters, the prophetic enthusiasm of Ruskin and the titanic energy of Morris, is not what the public have thought it to be: a nursery for luxuries ... for the rich. It is a movement for the stamping out of such things by sound production on one hand and inevitable regulation of machine production and cheap labour on the other ... The men of this movement ... want to determine the limitations of the factory system, to regulate machinery, to get back to realities in labour and human life.

Ashbee had founded the Guild of Handicraft in the east end of London for the education and training of young craftsmen. He moved the entire community to Chipping Campden in 1902 where it lasted until 1907. It failed there because it was too far from its markets, but the tradition lived on and Paul Woodroffe, though not a member of the Guild, was a gifted and successful artist, made slightly uneasy by the discovery that my father was already a

6

member of the Art Workers' Guild and in effect an established artist himself.

More significant was the fact that Woodroffe had two boys who needed a tutor. The tutor, already there, was Kathleen Clarke, who had come from Ireland. She was a most determined woman, small and red-haired, fantastically energetic and quick-witted. She had been a student of DeValera's in University College, Dublin and became a member of the Sinn Fein party at the time of the Easter Rising of 1916. It was she who persuaded my father to set up on his own. They were married in 1924.

In many ways, my mother was the very opposite of my father. Where he had left school at the age of fourteen, she was a student at the national university in Dublin where she had studied mathematics. She was a brilliant mathematician with a prodigious memory; she also read and translated from the Latin. She dominated every gathering she went to and took instant likings and dislikings to people she met. To judge from my father's stories and recollections, she must have been a difficult and tempestuous companion. I doubt if he was ever in love with her but he respected and was devoted to her. He recalled how on one occasion when she was organising a garden festival in the local village hall, all of the plants, vegetables, flowers and fruit had been listed and labelled, when a gust of wind blew all the labels away. She put her mind to it and remembered every item, its description and value – and made not a single mistake. She was ill for several days afterwards.

Accounts of her background and early life do not tally well and I remain vague about her record. As I understood it from my father and various friends and relatives, she had been educated at a convent school, went to university in Dublin and became enthused with the cause of Irish independence. The farmhouse in which she had grown up was raided by the notorious Black and Tans and she was frog-marched into the farmyard with a pistol in her back. After that, during the subsequent Civil War in Ireland, her father persuaded her to go for safety to England.

7

My recollection of her is of a short and rather stout lady with red hair in a bun which fell down below her waist on the few occasions she untied it. She sang Irish songs, played the fiddle and talked with great vivacity and certitude. She had grown up on a farm, Possextown, near Nobber in County Meath. Her father was described as a gentleman farmer; he was also a Justice of the Peace. He was six feet tall and one of six brothers all at least the same size. He had fallen in love with the daughter of a rich family, the Floods, who lived in a big ramshackle country house (now demolished). She had been captivated by the dashing gentle-man farmer on a horse, eloped with him, found herself in the kitchen of a farmhouse with no help and few neighbours and recognised that she had made the most dreadful mis-take. According to my father's account, she spent a whole night weeping, pulled herself together and never left the house again. She bore him five children. When I met her, she was a tiny, shrivelled old woman in her kitchen.

But here – in case it wasn't already obvious – I must insert some words about our religion. Both my father (with occasional doubts) and my mother (with no doubts at all) were Catholics – what are nowadays called 'Roman' Cath-olics. We did not use that geographical term; we were simply Catholics – that is, members of a universal church – which is what 'Catholic' means.

It was so much part of our life that it never ever occurred to me as a child that we might have been anything else. Catholicism had an ancient and continuous history; and it owed its origin to Christ's beloved apostle Peter, and as far as we were concerned it taught the truth; it knew what was right and what was wrong and made sure that we knew it as well. Attendance at Mass on Sundays was compulsory and we never missed it. On the only occasion I remember as a small boy refusing to go, my mother took out a stick and caned me on the bottom.

In 1936 my father and mother decided that we ought to visit Ireland and see the farm where she had been born and grew up. My father had bought his first car, an Austin

7, a few years previously and followed it with a strange saloon called a Jowett. It seemed to resist being started. My first acquaintance with swear-words was when my father tried to 'wind it up' to start it in the mornings. To celebrate and give some certainty on our visit to Ireland he bought a new car, an Austin 12, square and black and shiny. In the narrow, half-tarred roads of rural Ireland it seemed outrageously smart and prosperous. But the farm we thought was great. The cows were milked by Paddy Rooney, the dairy was run by Aunt Baby, my mother's youngest sister, with whom my father fell in love. She had been unwell for many years, had only one lung and died shortly after we returned to England.

The news of her death arrived by a telegram read to my mother on the telephone. She did not hear it all but screamed and sobbed as soon as she heard the fatal words. Sitting upstairs with my brother Mickie in our bedroom we heard the noise, realised something was seriously the matter and having a gramophone record with the repetitive chorus 'Cheer up, cheer up', we put it on loud in the hope that it would help. Dad came bounding up the stairs, tore the record off the machine and smashed it to pieces.

By that time my father and mother had moved from the house at Whiteleaf to a large ramshackle and at first somewhat derelict house with a large garden in North Dean, four miles from High Wycombe in the Chiltern Hills. There my father built up a considerable business as a stained-glass artist. He had a small team of craftsmen working in his studio, by now a large and spacious building with a wall totally glazed on the north side. The chief assistant was Gilbert Sheedy, the glass painter Mr Gadsby, the glazier a Mr Castell. They talked a lot, but not when my mother was present. They were encouraged by her to visit the kitchen twice a day for tea and were quickly sent back to get on with their work – a situation that never happened again after my mother's death.

The house in North Dean was the ideal setting for a lively childhood. It was called Lady Margaret Cottage, long and rambling, with two staircases and a huge open fireplace in the middle room. The garden was about four acres with a well, fruit trees and a meadow. We had a cat and lots of chickens, and we enjoyed ourselves pretending to drive cars round the garden and through its tall stinging nettles. We had a maid, Rose, and a gardner. In the evening there was music, sometimes a trio with Dad at the piano.

Although the 1930s are generally described as the years of the Depression, it seems not to have affected my father's work. The studio was busy and visitors came and went. They included artists like Stanley Spencer whose brother Gilbert had for many years been a friend of my father's; I remember the two Spencers and my father talking endlessly in the studio. All three told me later that the others spoke so much they couldn't get a word in edgeways.

We had holidays by the seaside, usually in Norfolk. And once we had a car, we visited friends in an expanding neighbourhood or drove to my parents' fond meeting place, Chipping Campden.

I had learned to read (I am told) at the age of two, often reading my mother's newspaper upside-down. We went to school at St Bernard's Convent in High Wycombe, which had adopted the 'Montessori method' of teaching for the smallest children. Mickie and I had various illnesses – pneumonia and pleurisy for Mickie, swollen glands for me. But generally it was a very happy and exciting time for all of us.

In 1937, my father and mother decided that my elder brother Michael (Mickie) and I should go away to boarding school – a Catholic school, of course. They considered a number of places and decided upon Ratcliffe College, run by the Rosminian Fathers (the Institute of Charity). Its prep. school was Grace Dieu Manor in Leicestershire. There we were sent in the Autumn of 1937. It was a devastating experience at that age and one to which I have never subjected my own children. Apart from a visit shortly afterwards, we never saw my mother again. For she died of kidney failure during that first term, on 10 December 1937.

10

I was seven years old; my brother was nine. We had both been homesick for several weeks. My brother never really ceased to be homesick; I, on the other hand, learned before the year was out how to be a member of a school community. We should never have been there at that early age; perhaps my mother had some inkling of what was to happen.

More than twenty years later I discovered that I could remember the whole day, even the ordinary events of the morning before they told us about her death. I remember getting up early for the daily Mass, and the maids helping me to put on my overcoat (a rather hairy green coat), and Eleanor, the clothes supervisor, being extra careful and talking quietly to the matron, Miss Robinson. Looking back on it, I realised that they must have been talking about me and my brother Mickie and knew that something was awry.

Then after breakfast, while we were in the classroom of Form I, someone came to the door and told us to come downstairs to the headmaster's study where he wanted to see us. His study was a small, narrow room opening directly off the main corridor. We walked nervously in and were met by the headmaster, Fr Francis O'Malley. He was obviously (I still remember) ill at ease.

We stood side by side just inside the door with our hands at our sides, not being allowed to put them in our pockets, and Fr O'Malley walked up and down in his black cassock. Then he turned to us and said that he had some very serious news for us.

'You know your mother has been very ill.'

'Yes,' we said.

'Well,' he went on after a long pause, 'she was very ill indeed. And now she's gone to heaven.'

We said nothing. I looked at Mickie. We looked back at Fr O'Malley.

'You know what I'm saying, don't you?' he went on. 'Your mother has gone to heaven.'

We said nothing. He began to look anxious; he walked up and down again, picked up a pipe and put it down again, walked back and stood in front of us and said again, 'You do understand what I'm saying, don't you? You know what I mean.'

'Yes,' I said. He looked even more baffled and stood right in front of us.

'Well,' he said, 'what do I mean?'

I said, 'I don't know.'

Fr O'Malley stopped walking up and down and stood still leaning over towards us.

'Then I'd better tell you simply. You know your mother was ill. She became worse. They took her to hospital a week ago. Last night she died. She is dead. Her soul has gone to heaven. You will never see her again.' We remained silent. 'I'll tell you what,' he said after a pause, 'why don't we go to the chapel and say a prayer for her?' He wrapped his great cloak with the lion's head clasp around him and led us to the chapel. I don't know what Mickie said to himself. I tried to say a prayer but couldn't think of anything to say. Then he led us out of the chapel and said, 'You can both have the rest of the morning off. Go to the playroom.'

As we walked away from him down some steps and along what seemed a long corridor (I have seen it since and, of couse, it is quite short), I looked back and saw Fr O'Malley twisting his cloak and its buckle and looking baffled and shaking his head.

Our lockers in the playroom were side by side. I looked into mine while Mickie looked into his. I thought it would be a good thing to cry, but I couldn't cry. I think Mickie also tried to cry and couldn't. We stood there getting more and more embarrassed and had nothing to say. Then we went back to the classroom.

Twenty-five years later, in my early thirties, when I was on the edge of a serious nervous breakdown and had even considered committing suicide, I thought I might be able to sort out my chaotic emotions and fears if I tried to trace and remember the events of my early years. In the middle of the night I drove out of the city where we then lived, up a hill to the moors, stood beside the car in the cold air and started tracing my story. That was when I suddenly realised that I could recall all the incidents of the day we were told of my mother's death. That night beside the car, I wept the tears that I should have shed twenty-five years before, sobbing and choking and crying aloud until the fit passed and the memory died away. It was not a total cure; that (as I shall explain in a later chapter) depended upon other events. But it was the start of a cure. It could not be a bad thing to remember and come to terms with the really devastating moments in one's life.

For the time being – and indeed for most of my life – that disaster had no effect upon my religious faith, and even less upon what is usually defined as the second 'cardinal virtue': hope. I occasionally think that, for me, hope is a kind of occupational disease. Later disasters, as we shall see, did not destroy that optimism. But I think it started during that first term at Grace Dieu Manor, when I was told about my mother's death. What could possibly be more devastating and shattering?

I went back to Grace Dieu Manor many years later, walked down the corridor and sat in the classroom remembering the day and writing it all down. I realised that my father had made a serious mistake in not fetching us from school to go to the funeral. We had no evidence of her death other than Fr O'Malley's interview. When we got home at the end of our first term, for Christmas, the only difference was that Mummy was not there. We walked over the hills to see her grave in the beautiful churchyard at Little Hampden and for many years afterwards, Mickie and I and one of our two sisters Joan and Anne walked over to it on Boxing Day and said some prayers. Mickie and I stayed at Grace Dieu Manor for three years. Joan was sent briefly to a boarding school at Stone run by Dominican nuns. Anne spent a few terms in the little school run by Eric Gill – and then moved to another convent school at Stroud also run by Dominican nuns.

The Fr O'Malley of whom I have just written should never, I thought later, have become a priest. He celebrated

Glasyers Studio and part of house

Mass every morning on his own, speaking in Latin so fast that no ordinary server could follow him. Mickie and I had learned to speak fast by listening to Dad who was a compulsive talker at top speed. So we took it in turns to serve Fr O'Malley's Mass and had a lonely breakfast afterwards.

Shortly after my mother's death, Fr O'Malley decided to become a sculptor. He carved a few small items and then landed a superb commission by being invited to carve a great hanging crucifix for the entry to the choir at Mount St Bernard's Abbey. The Cistercian monks had set up the abbey a few miles away on the other side of Charnwood Forest. We all walked there once a year and otherwise visited it with our parents. Having finished the great rood screen crucifix, Fr O'Malley tired of sculpture and became a brilliant photographer. Then he tired of that and became a psychiatrist. He moved from Grace Dieu to the Rosminian house at Ely Place in the City of London, became a chaplain to part of the university and studied psychology. He was a brilliantly quick-witted Irishman, who could do almost anything but never did enough to become master of it. Except possibly the photography. My father having lots of black hair, O'Malley made some superb portraits of him. (Incidentally, my father kept his hair, black and then grey and white, until he died at the age of ninety).

Grace Dieu dominated our lives. On the edge of Charnwood Forest and dominating a clearing that now contains football pitches and a cricket pitch, it was a handsome mostly nineteenth-century mansion restored by the local landowners, the DeLisles, with a chapel by the phenomenally productive architect and writer, A.W.N. Pugin. It was a beautiful representative home for the Second Spring of the Catholic faith. The DeLisles had been converts of the Rosminian fathers who came to England from Italy as a missionary team aiming at the conversion of England and saw schooling as the way to achieve it. Their main school was Ratcliffe College, to which we moved later; the prep. school, Grace Dieu, was smaller and more beautiful. Pugin designed Ratcliffe, which was built on a clear site. Grace

Dieu was an existing building, a manor house built after the dissolution of a convent in the sixteenth century.

Whatever may have happened to the other boys in the school, the lives of my brother Mickie and me were dominated by our unusual headmaster, Fr O'Malley. He was of middle height, lean and rather sallow, with black hair and a chin that always looked unshaven. My father and he became friends. Dad frequently came to Grace Dieu to stay, and talk, and talk, and talk.

A year after my mother's death, my father decided to move house. He left the house in the village of North Dean, bought a few acres at the top of the hill above it and built a new house and studio. There were a number of advantages. If the four of us as children had frequently been unwell in the valley, all of us (and there were eventually twelve) were remarkably fit at the top of the hill. It was a badly designed house but had an excellent studio. And across a few fields and hedges were the former farm buildings of Pigotts, owned and occupied by Eric Gill and his extended family.

Pigotts was a smallish farm on the flat top of a hill whose slopes were on all sides a forest of beech trees. When I first knew it, Pigotts was a quadrangle of buildings with a house down one side, barns and sheds on two sides (used as workshops), what later became a school building on the other side and a pigsty in the middle. Gill transformed the corner between his house and his own studio into a chapel and kept a chaplain.

These chaplains were, in themselves, extraordinary people, usually in some kind of disgrace. The first one I remember was Father Bernard McElligott, who was on leave from Ampleforth Abbey for reasons which were unclear to me at the time, and only a little clearer now. The second, whom I remember very well indeed, was Dr Flood. He was short and stout and bald. He had been a brilliant student of philosophy and was an expert on St Thomas Aquinas. He had been drummed out of Glasgow by the Bishop and found a welcome shelter in Gill's house. He was usually drunk. For several years, as a boy, I ran up to Pigotts in the morning to serve his Mass and usually had to wake him in his room above the chapel. In my simple innocence, I thought that the smell in the room was that of all priests; in fact it was the smell of stale beer. He was once seen with a notoriously drunken local driving a pony and trap through the village of North Dean and singing. A few years later he was found walking in the woods one morning when he had forgotten who he was. He eventually emigrated to Australia, lived there happily, I believe, and died, not in the odour of beer, but of sanctity.

The notoriously drunken local was Norman Ridgley, who had married Ishbel Macdonald, the daughter of Ramsay Macdonald, the first Labour Prime Minister. After her mother's death she had acted as hostess at 10 Downing Street and also at Chequers, the Prime Minister's country residence in Buckinghamshire, not many miles from where we lived. The Prime Minister set her up as the owner of the Plow Inn between Speen and Hampden. In my teens I walked with my brother and sister and friends to the Plow, where we were always welcomed and entertained by the incomparable Ishbel. Everyone thought it was a lovely idea for the Labour Prime Minister's daughter to marry a working-class man, but why that particular working-class man, who was already a notorious drunk, was incomprehensible. Sometimes, looking across the bar, we could see him lying unconscious on the floor. Eventually he grew a great boil on his nose, fell over and burst it and died. Ishbel returned to Lossiemouth in Scotland where she had been born and married the local chemist who had been a childhood friend. I called on her years later; she remembered us well.

Eric Gill was for many people – and certainly for Catholics with a social conscience – more than an artist. He was a social reformer who had founded a community – what he later called 'a cell of good living'. That was at Ditchling, inland from Brighton and easily reached by train and bus. On Ditchling Common, not far from the village of Ditchling where Gill's family at first lived, he started the community, the Guild of St Dominic, guided and inspired by the Domin-

17

ican friar Fr Vincent McNab. All its members were engaged in the arts and crafts: sculptors, engravers, printers, painters and potters. The day was punctuated by services and prayers, meals were at first in common, visitors flocked to see them and work with them.

As far as the Gills were concerned, the community came to an end when Eric Gill quarrelled with Hilary Pepler, who had been the joint founder of the Guild of St Dominic. The Gills moved to Capel y ffin in the Black Mountains of Wales, where an Anglican monk, Fr Ignatius of Llanthony, had built in the late nineteenth century a wonderfully simple and beautiful monastery, now empty. (It was later run as a guesthouse by Gill's daughter Betty who married one of Pepler's sons). From there, needing to be closer to London and the markets for work, they moved to Pigotts in the Chiltern Hills in Buckinghamshire.

Pigotts rippled with the coming and going of many fascinating and often eccentric apprentices and helpers – sculptors, engravers, printers. Gill's son-in-law, Denis Tegetmeier, whose family lived on the next hill (Denner Hill) and who had found Pigotts for the Gills, was a tall, thin and handsome man who was in many ways an isolate. He and his wife Petra produced a numerous family with four beautiful daughters whose attractiveness and popularity made that impossible. At the entrance to his studio was a huge placard with impeccable lettering: 'Leave my bloody tools alone'.

It was only many years later, with the publication of Fiona McCarthy's book on Eric Gill in 1988, that we learned about Gill's more bizarre habits. He had not only made love to his sisters and various friends, he had also had sex with his daughters. Being about the same age as most of his grandchildren, I grew up with them and I am sure – and have confirmed with them – that they had no idea of those incestuous activities. He left forty volumes of diaries (sold to a Californian university) which recorded his daily activities in brief detail and his sexual adventures in a code which he himself explained in the margin.

By the time we knew him, Gill was already hugely

successful as a sculptor, writer and typographer. His first major commission had been the Stations of the Cross for Westminster Cathedral. He then carried out innumerable commissions and even more gravestones. The lettering on both the carvings and the gravestones was superb and celebrated. It was the managing director of the Monotype Corporation who had the brilliant idea that Gill could also design typefaces. Of those typefaces (with which I am very familiar) the most attractive are Perpetua and Joanna, the most popular and widely used is Gill Sans – a 'Sans Serif' typeface similar to that designed for the London Underground by Gill's teacher, Edwin Johnston.

One of Gill's best known sculptures is the figure of Prospero with Ariel above the entrance to the BBC headquarters in London. The most extraordinary carving was the War Memorial for Leeds University of 1922, at first outside on University Road and later (when it had begun to suffer from the weather) in the entrance lobby of the main lecture hall. It shows Christ driving the moneylenders (in modern clothes) out of the temple. The staff and students of Leeds University have never understood why that episode was chosen, especially in a city known for its Jewish financiers. For me and for many visitors, the most romantic carving was the big flat crucifix fixed to a tall tree far into the woods that surrounded Pigotts. It was something more than a religious gesture or a statement of faith. Even as a boy I was conscious of some elemental meaning, some strange identity of a man and his saviour and the ultimate reality of living nature.

It all seemed so natural and happy. As children we played in and around Pigotts and explored the woods and felt the same magical unity with God and nature as Eric Gill must have felt when he nailed that crucifix to a tree in the wood. At the corner of the Pigotts quadrangle, linking on one arm to the house and the other to the workshops, the chapel was the spiritual hinge of our lives. The children sat or knelt in a row behind the altar and watched the sacred drama as a common event. On one occasion, I remember, one of them gave a running commentary throughout the Mass; the priest nearly choked when at the priest's communion the clear voice said, 'Now he's going to eat it!'

There was sometimes an amusing lack of dignity. One Sunday, as my father offered the tin of hosts and the dish for anyone who took a host as a sign of going to communion, Gill's son-in-law René Hague said, 'No thanks. I'd rather have a ham sandwich.' My father shuddered between shock and laughter.

I find it almost impossible to describe, still less explain, this relaxed acceptance of religious faith and natural irreverence. Religious ceremonial is after all fundamentally absurd, inviting laughter. We occasionally discussed whether God had a sense of humour (no evidence) and, if He had, was laughing in paradise, notably at the pretentiousness of the churches. Perhaps we were rather smug, with the confidence of knowing how absurd it could be.

Gill was himself the most attractive man. He was short, had (as I knew him) grey hair and a beard, never wore trousers but a knee-length woven smock, girded with a leather belt. He wore grey knee-length socks on weekdays and pink socks on Sundays. It was, he said, the correct and traditional garb for an artist and workman. He served Mass every Sunday in the chapel and did so beautifully. Visiting priests thought they had rarely if ever met a more spiritual person. His death was described by the priest who attended him as the most beautiful and holy death he had witnessed. He died in 1940 at the age of fifty-eight, having, through hard work and constant chipping of stone, developed lung cancer. He carved his own gravestone with the simple inscription 'Pray for me', 'Eric Gill' and the date of his birth; the date of his death was added by his assistant, Laurie Cribb.

My last memory of Eric Gill was, it now seems to me, in every way typical. A group of us were sitting on the grass of the tennis court shortly after the outbreak of the Second World War. Gill came back from London. He was in his usual artist's clothing with one addition. Because of the danger of air raids we were required to carry gas masks. In those days they were folded into a square cardboard box hung on a cord from the shoulder. Gill had one and we were surprised. We asked him if we could have it. Of course, he said, and threw it to us. We opened the box and it was empty. He walked away laughing.

My father was devoted to him, even though Gill himself did not like stained glass; as a sculptor trained in architecture, he wanted as much clear light as possible to come directly into a church. In contrast to Gill's studio and the stonecarvers' workshops, my father's new studio was ablaze with colour. He called it Glasyers, the mediaeval word for a glazier. It had – and still has – an enormous window facing north, ample room inside and workshops on both sides for cutting, glazing, firing and cementing. I learned to cut glass and paint it; later I learned to glaze it.

When we moved up the hill, my father's main assistant as a glass painter and craftsman was still Gilbert Sheedy, who later set up on his own but died young of a heart attack. The studio was always cold but wonderfully light. The four acres of ground around the studio and house were bare when we arrived and then began to change. My father planted everything: trees, bushes, flowers, vegetables. One of the most attractive features was a wooden table at the front of the house, built around an apple tree.

In 1939, my father, having for a short time been engaged to a girl who sang folk songs in a family group, married Daphne Reid who came from a very respectable middle-class family. Her father had been a senior officer in the Indian Civil Service; one of her brothers, Pat Reid, who became a prisoner of war after the invasion of France by the Germans in 1940 and to whom I wrote regularly at Oflag 4G, later became famous as the author of *The Colditz Story*, based on his experiences as the organiser of escapes from Colditz Castle.

Meantime our lives had changed in lots of ways. One of the groups we got to know were the 'Stribs'. That was short for Distributism, the social theory expounded by G.K. Chesterton and very attractive to artists and craftsmen, especially members of the Catholic church. Eric Gill spoke highly of it but as far as I know never joined the group. My father became a local representative and organised meetings in High Wycombe addressed by Chesterton. As a young man (or possibly as a boy, he did not specify a date), my father had been introduced to a book that he always spoke of as a definitive influence on his life. That was Thoreau's *Walden* or *Life in the Woods* published in 1854 and a best seller in its time. It described Thoreau's experience in retreating to 'The Pond' in 1845 where he lived 'the simple life'.

The simple life was then and for many years an idea very attractive to intellectuals, especially if they had plenty of money. My father did not have plenty of money, only what he earned. So he was never in a position to live it wholeheartedly. On the other hand, he could live the simple life of an artist-craftsman with no capital and no expensive tastes. He did not need holidays, drank an occasional glass of beer and dressed very simply, for most of the day in a blue smock appropriate for a stained-glass studio. His hair was rather long, the elbows of his jacket patched.

The Stribs, or followers of Distributism, were artistic people who had decided to try the simple life, preferably in a community. What could be simpler than cultivating the land and doing so unpretentiously, not as rich landowners but as a community? The 'back to the land' enthusiasts founded colonies in several parts of the country. The one we came to know best was at Laxton in Northamptonshire. Occasionally my father would drive us there to engage, not in the drudgery of farming, but in protracted conversations about life and work and art and, of course, God. Even as a child I was surprised that people could go out farming in open sandals.

My stepmother Daphne Reid had been educated at a convent in Belgium. Then she became a student at the Royal College of Art in London and from there – for reasons I never really understood – joined the land colony at Laxton, working in the household of Dunstan Davidson, who managed to run his part of the collective farm longer than anyone else. Another participant was Anthony Foster, one of Eric Gill's leading assistants, a brilliant woodcarver, married to the sister of the girl to whom my father had been briefly engaged. Friends of the land colony, the Murrays, who in High Wycome ran a group of anti-war pacifists called Pax, brought Daphne to the studio to see my father's work. They were soon engaged, married and spent a brief honeymoon at Capel y ffin, the former monastery owned by Eric Gill.

Against such a background, it was not altogether surprising that, in the years leading up to and after the declaration of war in 1939, Glasyers became a place of shelter (and occasionally work) for pacifists who were about to face (or had already faced) a tribunal as 'conscientious objectors'. My father's pacifism had nothing to do with his German ancestry; it was a natural and Christian result of his years in the prison camp during the Great War and his total disbelief in the declarations at the start of a war only twenty years after the disasters and absurdities of the last one. Convinced of the utter futility of war and the probable disasters of this one, he refused to listen to the news on the wireless and took no newspapers.

'Conshies' came to live either with us or at Pigotts (Eric Gill died in 1940 shortly after the outbreak of war). For us children the most delightful and entertaining character was a young man who was employed to dig the garden and had obviously no idea of the difference between vegetables and weeds. That was Victor Avico. After a year or two he got bored and joined the navy (I think) and died in Iceland. For him we made some superb glove puppets and he gave a hilarious Punch and Judy show in the studio (we had all moved there after letting the house). He also told us as children long stories of mythical characters like Dogsbody (which I remembered years later and told to my own children).

Pigotts was theoretically still a farm, and conscientious

objectors, who had been allowed to avoid military service provided they worked on a farm, became farm labourers. They included Walter Shewring, the senior classics master from Ampleforth College, a brilliant translator of Greek myths and Homer and a gifted pianist and organist. His problems climbing a stile or leading a horse gave us constant delight. Others included a very lively former apprentice of Gill's, Michael Richey, whose brother was a famous R A F pilot and who later (having like Victor found agriculture boring) joined the Merchant Navy and worked in it with notable bravery. Whatever some 'conshies' said about suffering from 'sheer funk', most of the ones I met were men of courage and self-sacrificing conviction.

Meantime our own fortunes changed dramatically. Daphne soon bore eight children (four boys and four girls) so that ultimately the family numbered twelve: four children of the first marriage and eight of the second. But the war had already caused many other changes.

Its outbreak did not surprise us. I remember (I was eight at the time) the news when Mr Chamberlain flew back from a meeting with Adolf Hitler and said there would be 'peace in our time'. My father said that there would obviously be another war. He and my mother had become English, for he had no wish to spend another war in an internment camp.

Meantime no one bought stained-glass windows. We therefore had no money; so my father offered to take us away from Ratcliffe College. Perhaps because I was a clever boy or possibly because of our misfortunes, the college allowed us to stay on as scholarship boys (from a fund, I was told later, for the children of impoverished Irish parents). We paid no fees but were charged for any extras. Our clothes got shabbier and shabbier. My brother Mickie never conquered his homesickness at the start of every term and never became an active member of the school. I, in contrast, threw myself into its life and work with determination. I was always first in the class, played cricket and rugger and became, at the age of twelve, Captain of the Junior School.

At home the outbreak of the war in 1939 changed everything. There were no further commissions for stained glass. To make our own contribution to the war effort, my father bought a pig and two goats. I tried (unsuccessfully) to milk the goats. The pig was housed in a sty converted from a room directly beneath our attic bedroom; the smell was formidable.

But we could not afford to stay at Glasyers. By a piece of good fortune, at the top of the next hill at Walter's Ash was the headquarters of what became Bomber Command. My father let the house to a succession of senior officers: Wing Commanders, Squadron Leaders, Group Captains, all of whom had flown over Germany and were subsequently promoted to a management job. One became eventually Head of the Royal Air Force, another became Head of the Indian Air Force.

We ouselves set off to distant parts of the country. At first we rented a cottage at Winterborne Whitchurch in Dorset (which I remember being full of fleas) and moved from there to a beautiful shepherd's cottage at Roke Down near Bere Regis where we painted the walls with colourful figures and religious scenes. Thence (when the farmer recruited a new shepherd) we moved to Roke Farm, wading through yards of manure to reach it.

After that, we moved to Gloucestershire, to a handsome stone house near Bisley. From there we could bicycle to Cheltenham or Gloucester or the nearest town, Stroud. My father, being over military age, was not called up; instead he did any work which came his way. From time to time, he would be a farm labourer or a bricklayer. After a few years we moved back to Glasyers, living in the studio throughout the rest of the war.

By that time my father had discovered a way of making money, using the skills which he would otherwise employ in making stained-glass windows. Both he and my stepmother decorated ordinary white plates, cups and saucers with colours made permanent by firing them in the stained-glass kiln, and sold them through local shops. Particularly popular and profitable was a plate with the badge of the American 8th Army Air Force in the centre and 'Enland 1940' round the edge. I quickly learned to apply lettering in my father's style, and design armorial compositions. We seemed to be back in business and making a satisfactory living.

Then, without warning, a disaster struck which changed the whole of my life. In October 1942, as Captain of the Junior XV at school, I walked off the rugby pitch with a terrible pain in my back and within a day was totally paralysed from the chest down. That game of rugby was the last time I ever ran. One other boy had already been taken ill. Panic spread; it was thought to be an epidemic. The school was closed for several weeks.

After several agonising days in the school infirmary, I was shifted to the general hospital in Leicester and from there, five weeks later, moved with the other boy to St Vincent's Orthopaedic Hospital in Middlesex. It was a remarkable place – a charity hospital which started, I believe, as 'Father Hudson's Cripples Home'. It was run by the Sisters of Charity of St Vincent de Paul, recognised by their voluminous blue dresses and huge white starched headdresses based upon French peasant headgear.

This was during the 1940s, before the foundation of the National Health Service. Poor people who could not afford medical help usually joined what was known as 'the panel' and received (sometimes minimal) attention from the local doctor. Nearly all the patients in St Vincent's Hospital were panel patients; the consultants did their work for little pay. But the standards were high and the treatments regular, generous and unstinting.

Near Pinner and Northwood Hills, the hospital consisted of a scattered collection of open-air low buildings on the slope of a hill. The central ones were fairly modern; the wards were older, built either of timber or (the later ones) of brick. Because at the start it had coped mainly with people suffering from TB (tuberculosis) it was an open-air hospital. The TB patients had later been joined by people with osteomyelitis and infantile paralysis. There were a number of spastics. All were disabled, most of them permanently. In the open air we could hear the noise of flying bombs overhead and sometimes see the explosions.

Of the various wards, I got to know two. St Michael's housed boys between the ages of eleven and fifteen. Like the other wards it was in the open air; it had no front wall, only canvas curtains that could be closed in the event of an air raid. The beds were lined up against the back wall. It was a simple wooden structure, with toilets and a kitchenette in buildings at the back. By modern standards it was, I suppose, quite inadequate. In fact I enjoyed it. I was there for nearly two years, through two winters when the snow blew in on us and we were kept warm by metal hot water bottles stuffed into the sides of the bed.

But at first it seemed inauspicious. For many months I had no idea what was the matter with me; the doctors and teachers, and even my father, seemed to think it was best for patients like me not to know the name of the disease from which we were suffering. I learned after a while that it was called poliomyelitis, which in those days was not the common name for the disease, even though it was the correct medical one. It was only when a boy on the ward told me that I had infantile paralysis that it made sense. As it happened, I had read in the *Readers' Digest* an article about Sister Kenny in Australia, who had taught children with infantile paralysis to walk again. I decided to do the same. Meantime, I was stretched out horizontally on an iron frame with my legs in plaster.

Once a day an elderly nun, Sister Louise, struggled with my bed and wheeled me up the slope for massage in the gymnasium. In the mornings, Sister Josephine gave us schooling – essentially the three Rs. In the afternoon, we learned leatherwork or shorthand and later, when we could walk, worked in the tailor's shop, the boot shop or the splint shop. The majority of illnesses being TB of the spine or hips, osteomyelitis or poliomyelitis, we all had to be fitted with splints or other appliances. I worked in the tailor's shop, making blue trousers for wounded soldiers and airmen.

At least once a fortnight or, when possible once a week, my father came to visit me. Laden with books that he thought I ought to read (he thought I ought to read something better than Agatha Christie, every one of whose books I had devoured), he took his old red bicycle down the hill from Glasyers, rode across several hills to Great Missenden, took a train from there to Northwood Hills and then walked the last mile or two to the hospital in order to sit, sometimes in the freezing cold, beside my bed. After a few weeks we had very little to say to each other. But he never let me down. I have never forgotten it.

And there were compensations. A middle-aged man who walked with great difficulty round the wards suggested one day (since I was articulate and could write) that I should get in touch with the Baden Powell Organisation and found a Boy Scout troop. So I did so and recruited half the ward as Boy Scouts. Most of us could not walk but we could shout. We wore Scout caps on our heads, usually on our faces if we were lying on our backs, and studied subjects like tracking, tying knots and climbing. When I got back on my feet, I learned to climb trees using only my hands and arms because my legs were useless and, for many years afterwards, could climb a rope in a gym using only my arms.

Many years later, I gave a radio talk entitled 'All on the Same Level'. We were of course literally on the same level but there was another meaning to the phrase. It was an education in egalitarianism. I acquired before I got back to school a profound hatred of pretentiousness and pomposity. The only people I intensely disliked were the occasional posh visitors who were consciously kind and – I thought – talked down to us. I learned, and never forgot, how important it was to belong to a community.

Apart from being more literate than most of the other boys and helping to read passages from school books to boys who had problems with reading, there was another reason why I was noticeable. Something having gone wrong with my urinary system, the consultant ruled that I must sit up vertically. But this would conflict with my treatment stretched flat on a frame. The ingenious sister on the ward solved the problem by having me tied to the frame and the frame tied to the bed – and the whole bed tilted onto its end. Then they put a table up against me. I could now survey the whole ward. Visitors thought it very odd and rather funny. I did not always appreciate the joke. Sometimes, when the blood sank down to my feet, I fainted.

Vertical or horizontal, after I had been in bed for about a year the doctors decided that it was time for me to walk again and had calipers fitted to both my legs. I also had a spinal support because my spine had become – and still remains – seriously twisted, with what is called 'scoliosis'. After several days of exercises, a determined nurse took me to the end of the ward, propped my back against the wall, took away my sticks and said, 'You are now going to walk.' It is quite difficult to swing one's legs in stiff calipers. I managed to get one round in front of me and then the other, and suddenly I knew I could walk. I swung my legs round one after the other until, with no warning, the floor came up and hit me on the nose. Having no sense of balance I had no sense of falling but lay there laughing uproariously, because I knew that I would, sooner or later, walk again.

And walk, I did.

Occasionally, as a group of walking patients, we went to the cinema. Most of us having calipers or splints on our legs, we sat in the front row and made no comments when people came past us in the dark and tripped over our legs. Their curses and their apologies gave us, I suppose, a few moments of unity with the outside world. In the hospital itself, some of us constructed a 'buggy', a sort of flat wheelbarrow which we became expert in pushing down the hill and at the last moment turning the corner in order to avoid a brick wall. A wounded air force patient who said he was an expert navigator insisted on our pushing him down the hill; of course, he went straight into the wall, smashed his wounded leg and was back in bed for a longer spell.

My own role was one that I had already discovered. When I was walking, even on splints, I helped to organise games. There was a small amount of land in front of the ward and we set up stumps and played cricket. It took many minutes for the bowler to reach his end of the crease and even longer for the batsmen to run but it was worth it and it was hilarious. I think even then I was learning to organise other people. I left hospital at the age of fourteen, with a caliper on one leg and my torso still encased in plaster. For many years I returned as an outpatient and gradually changed the appliances: a back support of steel and leather and a half-caliper on one leg.

I returned to Ratcliffe College in the summer of 1944, bound together with a plaster jacket and a caliper on one leg. I spoke with a Cockney accent and entertained my friends with Cockney rhyming slang. The College corrected my accent by getting me to read the bible at breakfast. In addition, the school lost no time in getting me involved in activities which they said (rightly) would be good for me. The 2nd Eleven was notorious for its failure at cricket. I was made its captain and since I could not run was provided with a runner. In my first game the runner was run out. I decided to give up cricket and take up rowing. It never crossed my mind that if I fell into the water my plaster jacket would sink me.

My record in school lessons was of a different order, partly because of my native cleverness and partly because I could not now play sports. I decided – admittedly only for a short time – to devote myself to scholarship. I could already spell complicated words. Now I worked out how to learn enough to pass examinations. I never failed an exam but loved taking them. At the end of my first year after returning, I won not only first prize for the class but the prize for every subject. Nothing could have been more frustrating for my fellow pupils. I also took part in many other intellectual activities: debates, plays, concerts. The Debating Society met every Sunday evening and debated either serious propositions or flippant ones. My main opponent was often Norman St John Stevas (now Lord St John of Fawsley) who learned his debating skills in that society. When, at the end of the war, during the national election, we held school political elections, Norman was the Conservative candidate and I was the Labour agent. He won by an overwhelming majority.

Of the teachers who most influenced my life, the most important were the President of the College, Fr Cuthbert Emery and the Prefect of Studies, Fr Murray – known as 'Chimp' because of his wiry and agile appearance. During Fr Murray's reign the academic standards at Ratcliffe College reached heights not known before and, I believe, rarely matched later. Murray not only taught us Latin but had studied methodically the examinations set by the Oxford & Cambridge Joint Examination Board. As far as I can remember, no one failed in the three years during which I sat for the School Certificate and then the Higher Certificate. At that time, the maximum number of subjects permissible for the School Certificate was nine and you could be awarded either a pass, credit or distinction. So I set out to get nine distinctions and succeeded, despite frequent illnesses which included measles, pleurisy and scarlet fever. During a bad bout of measles, I was for nearly a fortnight both blind and deaf and spent my time remembering all the poetry I had ever learned. Fr Emery had encouraged us to learn as much poetry as we could. 'You never know,' he said, 'when you might find yourself stranded somewhere in the dark without books – like a station platform in wartime.' I had taken his advice and learned as much poetry and prose as I could absorb.

Even more significant was the man I first met when I decided to study German rather than physics. This was Walter Ullmann, an Austrian refugee to whom Fr Emery had given shelter before the war. It took us a few years to discover that Dr Ullmann was more than a German teacher; he was the most scholarly historian, a doctor of both Civil

31

and Canon Law, and he was writing a fundamental work on the mediaeval Empire and Papacy. He left Ratcliffe to take up a lectureship at the University of Leeds and from there moved to Cambridge where he became a Fellow of Trinity and finally Professor of Mediaeval History. He recognised, and later told me, that I would never be a great scholar, dedicated to research. 'You,' he said, 'will just read ten books and write the eleventh.' He was right.

His teaching – effectively lectures and tutorials – was a revelation. History was no longer dates and events and periods; it was a dispassionate study of thought. To take only one case, what was the Renaissance? No longer just the revival of ancient learning; it was a 'revolt against scholasticism'. For several years his typewriter could be heard clattering away through the night. Then he married and moved to a cottage nearby and his wife taught us English. In the sixth form we studied in the library. Provoked into discussions by both the Ullmanns we experienced the intellectual life of a university in a way that some of us never experienced again.

If Walter Ullmann intoduced me to a more profound understanding of history, his wife Elizabeth, who conducted what were effectively tutorials in the library, introduced me to modern literature. We studied many periods but in particular she persuaded us to read – and certainly to enjoy – the work of modern poets, especially T.S. Eliot. I learned many of his shorter poems by heart and devoured *Murder in the Cathedral*.

I decided to become a poet or a dramatist. My problem, shared by many potential authors before and since, was that I couldn't think of anything to write about. I produced a long poem about the origin and manufacture of the disgusting sausage-meat we ate during the war. It was unmistakably Eliotesque in style with shades of 'Webster was much possessed by death, And saw the skull beneath the skin'. I recognised that I was not a serious poet; but it was Elizabeth Ullmann's teaching me how to study poetry that had a major influence on my studies later at the University of Edinburgh.

What happened at home? The end of the war in 1945 meant that there was soon more than enough work in stained glass, for memorials and for restoration after bomb damage. The studio filled with young assistants and students. Our social lives were increasingly influenced by Pigotts and the Gills. Having discovered, despite my disabilities, how to ride a bicycle, I explored with family and friends many parts of Buckinghamshire and discovered many fascinating places and buildings. I fell in love with one of the beautiful Tegetmeier girls and spent a lot of time at Pigotts where in any case the stone workshops and the printing press were busy again. It all seemed lively, rather crazy and full of character – and certainly characters: artists, musicians, actors and writers.

The village of Speen further up the hill from North Dean seemed to be a den for writers and musicians. Among them was Edmund Rubbra, the composer, who wrote much of his best music there (and incidentally took over his neighbour's wife). His New Year's parties were brilliant and full of music.

Of the characters, I remember none more vividly than Mr Piercy, who lived a few miles away at Dunsmore and travelled by train to London every weekday to work as an engineer in the London County Council. My elder sister Joan married his son Bobby. Mr Piercy (known to his wife as Tinker) had worked abroad and returned to rural Buckinghamshire to grow food and collect things. At auctions he bought such treasures as school desks going cheap, lots of gloves (usually with one missing from the pair), every kind and size of nail and screw and at least three sets of the *Encyclopedia Britannica* (usually with one volume missing). He kept every copy of *The Times*, *Telegraph* and *Sunday Times* and stacked them in his bedroom so that ultimately he had to sleep outside in a tent.

Utterly convinced of the value of organic growth and manure he used only an earth closet and fertilised with its rich contents an acre of field which grew the most luscious fruits and vegetables I have ever seen; he grew so many huge marrows that no one in the village wanted them and he was reduced to leaving them on people's doorsteps in the night. Since he emptied his bowels before leaving in the morning he never used toilets in London and therefore brought home occasional rolls of toilet paper (labelled LCC). He noted every morning the temperature, barometric pressure and weather forecast and left a typed record for his wife. He also filed anything of interest, including his nail clippings in brown envelopes inscribed with 'Left Foot' or 'Right Foot' and the date. After his death it took many months to sort out his treasures. The acre continued to be the most fertile land in the county.

Back at school, I was introduced to drama and began acting in plays despite my disabilities, when they needed someone who could learn a particularly long and complicated part. After that I acted regularly in school plays, notably in Gilbert and Sullivan (I was a fairy in *Iolanthe* in my first year and Lord Chancellor in my last), and then set up the Ratcliffe Entertainment Committee (REC) to write and perform variety shows. They may have been despicable but we enjoyed ourselves even if the audiences had mixed views. And I never lost my enjoyment in acting. I acted at college and university and organised amateur (and later professional) dramatics.

It was time to decide on a career. Towards the end of my time at Ratcliffe College, I made a crucial (and I once thought disastrous) decision about my future. I had spectacular examination results: the subjects already mentioned, a Higher Certificate in less than one year (again interrupted by illness) with distinction papers taken less than a year later. The school and its advisers had no doubt that I should go to Cambridge and when, several years later, I saw Cambridge for the first time and discovered its beauty, I recognised (for a short time) what a mistake I had made. But at the time I was determined to become an architect – not any architect, but a *great* architect. The architecture course at Cambridge University was, at that time, not highly regarded, and it was thought by my teachers that a clever lad like me should not waste his time studying such a third-rate subject. In any case, I wanted to study architecture in a College of Art where I could also do some drawing and painting. Despite all my entrance qualifications, I was not particularly keen to go to a university.

In the end it was my father who made the decision. The artist for whom he had carried out a lot of very good stained glass was Herbert Hendrie, the Head of Design at Edinburgh College of Art. The Principal of the College, whom my father had known at the Royal College of Art, was Hubert Wellington, now retired and living in Buckinghamshire. We went to see him and, not very surprisingly, he recommended Edinburgh College of Art which had, he said, a very good school of architecture. I decided to try it and, to my surprise, was accepted on the basis of a single letter. It changed my life.

Why did I want to become an architect? I think now that it was really because of my love for old buildings, rather than a compulsive need to design new ones. Driven by my father every weekend, I had seen and admired cathedrals of different dates in Chichester and Liverpool and loved the Cotswolds and their architecture. I had visited dozens of parish churches; I had made drawings of the new cathedral at Guildford and had been immensely impressed by a Lutyens house, the Deanery at Sonning-on-Thames. I recognised much later that the love of old buildings was not enough. But I took advice from a stained-glass colleague of my father's who had worked at Edinburgh College of Art and set out upon my academic journey.

The first letter I received from my father told me that, the day after my departure, his studio had been burned down to the ground. In the ashes were all my books and belongings, all my prizes. I never saw them again. It was nothing to my father's loss, which included most of his early drawings and most of his photographs, including nearly all the pictures he had taken of my mother. For me it was not so much a disaster as a symbol. It seemed to be telling me that my adolescence was over. I could forget my childhood, my scholarship, my elementary learning, my disasters, my successes and most of my hard-won skills. I would start again – in a new, strange and wonderful city.

2

The Athens of the North

In the summer of 1948 I joined a party of schoolfellows from Ratcliffe for a bicycle tour of Scotland. With a school-friend (both of us on bicycles) I organised a lift on a lorry to join the rest of the team in Edinburgh. We spent our first night in a youth hostel divided between several tenements in the Lawnmarket at the top of the Royal Mile. It was semi-derelict and disgusting. The lavatory was the most revolting I had ever used. I wondered if all urban lavatories were like that. I had never slept in a city or a town before.

But that did not matter. I walked and rode into the city, down the High Street and up to the Castle, and was completely captivated. It was more fascinating, more dramatic, more overpowering than anything I had imagined. I came back and stayed in Edinburgh for fifteen years.

On that first visit, however, I was really on a tour of Scotland. And that was another unusual experience. We cycled north from Edinburgh to Perth, Pitlochry and then Inverness. There we turned, cycled south the length of Loch Ness and stayed in Fort William. We rode to Glencoe, took a boat across Loch Lomond and ended up after a few days in the Trossachs, by which time I was more exhausted than I had ever been before.

Our leader and guide was one of the school's masters, Br Tedesco. Back in Edinburgh he introduced me to relatives who were Italian Scots, descended from immigrants who had come to Scotland at the end of the nineteenth century. The Marble Arch Fish Restaurant was run by the di Ciaccas, the eldest boy of whom had been at Ratcliffe.

That tour around Scotland was invaluable. I arrived as a

37

Edinburgh from High Street c. 1950. Drawn while a student at Edinburgh

student at the Edinburgh College of Art having seen more of Scotland than many of my contemporaries, including some of the Scots. And some lessons were astonishing. One Saturday afternoon in Edinburgh we rode to the open square known as the Mound beside the Royal Scottish Academy, where soapbox orators entertain the public. A well-known town councillor delivered a scathing attack on Roman Catholicism. We heard that in the confessional, women were regularly seduced by the priest. The chief target of his attack was the elderly Canon Gray who, far from attacking women, had been a youthful friend of Oscar Wilde and is generally considered to be the original for *The Portrait of Dorian Gray*.

I was alarmed at the time that it might be a grievous mistake for a Catholic to enter a nest of hatred of Catholicism and its representative, the Pope. It took me a year or two before I began to understand the ambivalence of most of the Scots. 'You know,' said a Church of Scotland friend to me one day, 'why we write "Fuck the Pope" in the public lavatories? It takes too long to write "Fuck the Moderator of the General Assembly of the Church of Scotland".'

But back to the bicycle ride. We stayed in youth hostels every night. It rained every day. After a few days we abandoned our raincoats and cycled in vests and pants, drying out in the evenings and singing (mostly Gilbert and Sullivan) for several hours. It was a valuable introduction to Scotland and the beginning of a love affair – not uncritical but increasingly profound. And it was for me the start of a serious and continuing study of Scotland.

But for the moment, with or without a bicycle, my home was Edinburgh. What was Edinburgh to me, a stranger and an innocent discovering and living in a city for the first time?

I knew from the start, and certainly the next morning, when I rode my bicycle up to the Castle and down to Holyrood Palace, that this was a quite extraordinary, utterly dominating, arrogant and sometimes sinister place. The tall buildings seemed to lean over the roads and railway, and the railway ran through the very centre. Small, thickly-dressed men and women scurried up staircases in massive grey blocks of houses and flats and workrooms, their faces reddened by the wind, their expressions unwelcoming, impassive and private. I thought that the Old Town – the great crag and spine that forms the High Street and the Canongate (the Royal Mile) with its closes and wynds and tall unyielding masonry cliffs – was the whole of Edinburgh; and it still occupies my memories and fantasies, even years after I learned to know the eighteenth century New Town, the Victorian terraces and the modern suburbs.

I recognised that I had embarked on an endless journey and that the city – cold and black and smoky and resistant – would take over my life. I still cannot arrive in Edinburgh by train and walk up the slope from Waverley Station and look across at the tenements and the castle, without feeling breathless and rather frightened. At the top of that slope is the most preposterous monument ever erected to a single man: 200 feet of black Gothic arches, traceries and pinnacles imprisoning a shiny white statue of Sir Walter Scott.

I had of course come to Edinburgh to attend not its university but its College of Art. But before I describe my joining that proud institution, let me talk about some of the people I soon got to know and who affected the rest of my life.

Having always been a Catholic and attended a Catholic public school, I saw it as my duty to report as soon as possible to the university's Catholic society. That society in Edinburgh was known as the Catholic Students Union (CSU). It had two houses in George Square, one for the Union itself and the other for a Dominican priory, staffed by priests who conducted services and discussions and supplied the CSU. The prior was a shy and unpretentious man called Bernard Delaney. The assistant chaplain was a young Dominican, Fr Anthony Ross, who was to have a major influence on my life.

The common room of the CSU in George Square was a rather untidy, friendly place in which to relax and talk. It

Biddy Badenoch

had a library; its members were students of all colleges and all disciplines. I followed my usual habit of taking a sketchbook with me and making a few drawings of some subject that I have forgotton when a girl hurried in and rushed over to say something, kicking the open bottle of Indian ink that lay on the floor beside me and splattering the wall. She then ticked me off for putting it in such a dangerous place.

'Who is this bossy girl?' I asked of one of my companions.

'Her name is Biddy Badenoch,' he replied, 'and she lives next door.' I married her six years later.

That 'next door' was both the home and medical consulting rooms of Dr Badenoch, a most remarkable man. Alexander Guthrie Badenoch was to me more than a future father-in-law; he became a very close friend. His story was extraordinary. He had grown up in a very conventional Presbyterian family in Aberdeen, then volunteered for the army in the Great War. He was accepted with some difficulty, being small and very slight. The Gordon Highlanders found another man as small as he and between them they carried stretchers on the Western Front for several years, notably after the devastating battles of the Somme. He once told me that his partner, Tim Keith, was the bravest man he had ever met. The admiration was mutual. Tim Keith (who attended our wedding) told me that Dr Badenoch was the bravest man *he* had ever met!

After the Great War, Guth (as he was always known) decided to become a missionary. He had taken a degree in classics at Aberdeen University before the war; he now took a degree in medicine and became a medical missionary in Africa. On return from Africa he became a Roman Catholic, to the great distress of his family; his father was said to have been so ashamed that he never lifted his head up in public again. Guth then moved to Malaya as a medical officer of health in government service and was for a year in charge of a leper colony.

He returned to Scotland and was for many years the GP at Garelochhead, at the foot of the Clyde. He could almost have been the pattern for Dr Cameron, the senior doctor in

Dr Finlay's Case Book, which much later came to television. To be nearer the right schools he moved with his family to Edinburgh and took over a practice in George Square in a house which had been the childhood home of Walter Scott. Of his five daughters the one I fell in love with was the second, Biddy. I came to know the Badenochs very well; as well as sparkling company, they provided the finest breakfast on Sunday mornings I have ever eaten.

Dr Badenoch's knowledge of the classics never left him; he could make jokes in Latin and possibly in Greek, but since I knew no Greek, I had no way of judging his expertise. He read widely and was a good conversationalist. He was consulted on many subjects as well as medicine. Some people thought him eccentric, especially because he was an enthusiast for natural, organic fertilisation and kept compost heaps in his back garden, whose temperature he regularly checked. He was of course right; but he was ahead of his time.

The problem that ultimately destroyed his career was that he could not persuade himself that the National Health Service was right for the country or its citizens. Having myself been a patient in a hospital before the days of the NHS, I disagreed profoundly with him. He believed that as first conceived by Aneurin Bevan it would make for bad medicine. He survived for a time in George Square with what had been a specialist practice for many senior university staff; but as they gradually left the university or died they were not replaced and his income declined. Eventually at the age of fifty-three, he decided to emigrate to Canada, and sit his examinations again. He ended as deputy superintendent of a mental hospital in Nova Scotia. He had already, in Edinburgh, begun to study psychiatry and attended clinics conducted by a leading psychiatrist. He returned to Scotland and died at the age of sixty-seven. I was told that when he left for Canada he destroyed all his diaries, including those recording his work as a stretcher-bearer on the Somme. I deeply regret my failure to record his remarkable experiences.

Back in Edinburgh, in addition to the Badenochs, George Square was home to a number of remarkable people. Of the Dominican friars next door to the Badenochs, the one I came to know best was Fr Anthony Ross. Anthony had grown up in a staunchly Free Presbyterian family near Inverness and then been an undergraduate at Edinburgh University before becoming a Catholic, a priest and a friar. He was now supposed to be writing a Ph.D. thesis but never found enough time for it. He explained that the perpetual conflict between scholarship and social concern led him towards the latter.

After leaving Edinburgh, he was, for a time, prior at a monastery in Gloucestershire and a schoolmaster in Staffordshire, but then came back to Edinburgh and devoted himself to active work among prisoners and alcoholics. So celebrated was he in the area of social concern that the staff and students of the university elected him Rector, the Rector in a Scottish university being (on the pattern first developed in Bologna) elected by the students to be chairman of the University Court, the body that controls the money and discipline. It seemed extraordinary that a Dominican friar should have been elected chairman of the University Court in the city of John Knox. In fact it was a brilliant innovation. Anthony played an active role as Rector. He had already founded a Centre for Scottish Catholic historical archives in Edinburgh. After the Rectorial episode, the members of his order elected him Provincial. He then suffered a massive stroke, returned to Scotland, wrote part of his autobiography and died a few years later.

When I first met him, Anthony was playing a key role in the Catholic Students' Union. In a rambling university like that of Edinburgh, such societies were vital; they seemed more real than the University Union which never really became a socially viable unit. Anthony was a major influence, first in my student life and on many subsequent occasions. He persuaded a number of us to make a pilgrimage on the first Sunday of Lent to the Cistercian Abbey at Nunraw in the Lammermuir Hills, east of Edinburgh. It was

Lady Stair's House, Edinburgh, April 1949

45

a twenty-six mile walk and I failed to complete it three times. Anthony was an immensely strong man who carried my rucksack and eventually me. But he was more to me than that. He became, in effect, almost a foster-son in that house in George Square, next to the Dominican Priory, occupied by the Badenochs. Shortly after my graduation, when I married Biddy Badenoch, Anthony Ross performed the ceremony.

But that was long after. For the moment I must try to recapture the impression that crowded in on me as I became a student in Edinburgh College of Art. I had found some very respectable lodgings, but quickly moved – on Anthony Ross's advice – to cheaper lodgings in a less middle-class area. In those days, and certainly if you were at a college rather than a university, you had to find your own lodgings or 'digs'.

The College of Art occupied (and still does) some large red sandstone buildings erected at the end of the nineteenth century on the slope above the valley south of the famous ridge of the old city. It was an area I was to get to know very well indeed. But for the moment let me recapture those instant impressions of the College of Art in Lauriston Place.

It was not an auspicious start. In 1948 nearly all the students had been in the armed services, usually through conscription both during and after the Second World War. Having suffered from poliomyelitis and still supported by a back support and a caliper on one leg, I had been rejected at my medical examination for the armed services. All the other members of the First Year architectural course were ex-soldiers, sailors or airmen. When I limped into the studio, and enquired where I was to go, the first words addressed to me were 'Fuck off.' Wandering disheartened down a corridor I met a girl who had just attended the inaugural meeting of First Year Drawing and Painting students and been told, 'Let's be quite clear. You are the grey background against which the occasional genius might just possibly emerge.'

Bakehouse Close, Edinburgh, May 1949

47

Encouraged by such Scottish assurances, I went to the College shop and bought the drawing boards, squares and instruments I would need for my course. This was in the days (superseded in the fifties) when you were supplied with nothing and had to buy it all. Then I went back to the bare studio, claimed my share of a long table on which I could prop my drawing board and met, at the same time, the student who was to become my closest friend and share much of my student life. That was Dave Barnes.

John David Woodward Barnes, always known as Dave Barnes, was a cool, very English and apparently competent young man. He had started to study in Edinburgh, been recruited for national service in the army and been posted to Cyprus. His comments about the army were both funny and scathing; he seemed to have landed in a sea of corruption. But he was easy to know. In the First Year architectural studio of Edinburgh College of Art, he was for me a blast of refreshing fresh air.

He was not a gifted architectural designer and in the end he failed. But there was a different – and fascinating – side to him. It took me several months to discover that, beneath his cool and gentlemanly appearance, there lay a brilliant natural clown. That was important for another aspect of my student life. Having organised revues at school, I began to organise variety concerts in the college. Dave and I put on a joint act. Between us we dominated the concerts, with Dave as the clown and me as the straight man or 'feed'. He would climb anywhere, crawl anywhere; if you asked him to do a funny walk across the stage, he would produce a walk so absurd and grotesque that it brought down the house. He was a precursor of the hilarious absurdities of *Monty Python's Flying Circus*. As a performer, rather than architect, he became a household name – a college character.

Nothing could have surprised me more than the breakdown that occurred several years later. Dave had failed his studio work and many examinations. On one occasion a group of us fellow students worked for several nights to complete his designs and help him through. He still failed –

perhaps the teaching staff recognised the hands that had produced much of the work. Having left the College, he worked in several architects' offices and we kept in touch.

One evening he called on me, took me to the nearest tavern and suddenly asked me to go with him to South America and covert the people to Christianity. I thought at first it must be a joke, but in fact he was serious. I was, for various reasons, living on my own in a little flat in an impoverished tenement building. He slept there for several nights, snapping his fingers and telling me that he felt a desperate need to kill someone (I trusted it would not be me). During the day he seemed to be in a state of euphoria, walking unharmed through traffic while I hung back on the pavement. His condition rapidly deteriorated. He was diagnosed as a paranoid schizophrenic, spent time in a mental hospital and returned home to stay in the south of England.

But before I write about some of the other colourful characters I met in Edinburgh, I must linger in the College of Art and its School of Architecture. When I arrived, modern architecture had not completely taken over the curriculum. The teaching was traditional, based (if anything) on the model of the famous Beaux Arts system.

In the studio, we had exercises in lettering, perspective and skiagraphy. Lectures seemed to me elementary and I became aware of an increasing boredom. I took evening classes in antique drawing and clay modelling. During the daytime, I spent most afternoons wandering through Edinburgh and exploring alleyways, the 'closes and wynds' of the Old Town. Even on a cold Edinburgh day that seemed to me rewarding. Children would gather round whilst I was drawing and on more than one occasion danced for me. I still have many of those drawings.

The teaching staff in the College were invariably helpful and sometimes amusing. The Acting Head of the School, who later became its Head and Professor, was Ralph Cowan, a brilliant designer and quiet observer of the oddities of the social scene. The studio instructors in the First Year were local architects whose main interest or preoccupation was architectural practice. Ralph Cowan, Esmé Gordon and Harry Wylie became friends as well as instructors. But even with them and in conversation with them, I was aware of a growing intellectual emptiness. To put it simply, I could not find out what modern architecture was supposed to be about and what made it distinctive, different from that of any other architectural period.

If classical lettering and calculated perspective were (after the first year) discarded and forgotten, what were the springs of the new architecture? Not the styles, classical or Gothic; modern architecture had dispensed with them. It was bare, unpretentious and functional. We might not learn traditional styles and their details, but we learned how to *plan* better than ever before. In the studio we read our schedules of accommodation, designed buildings and prepared study sheets of building construction and building services. An artist known to us as 'the tree man' because he had been brought in to teach us how to draw trees (and thus improve our drawings) took us out sketching – where I came into my own.

But I never understood – and was certainly not told – what modern architecture was about. In 1952 I accompanied a friend, Gerard Walmesley (always known as Geoff Walmesley) to Italy. I sat on the pillion of his powerful motorbike and we drove through France and Switzerland, over the Pyrenees and spent two months exploring, visiting and occasionally sketching the monuments and sites of northern Italy. We visited Milan, Venice, Ravenna, Florence, Rome, Pisa and Siena and the hill villages of Tuscany, sleeping in the open (we did not have a tent) and studying the buildings I had painstakingly listed beforehand.

We saw and visited so many that after two months we began to suffer from what I called 'architectural constipation'. When we stopped our motorbike outside Pisa Cathedral and its famous Leaning Tower we decided that we would be physically sick if we visited another building; we remounted and drove away. But our studies were an unforgettable experience. More than any lectures and books

The Old Manor, Burton-on-Trent

51

and discussions, those two months gave me an unforgettable architectural education.

At Edinburgh College of Art social life was colourful. At the end of the Christmas term, the Art Revels took over virtually the whole of the College and we disguised it from top to bottom. Within a few months I became involved in writing and performing variety shows. More seriously, with a number of other enthusiasts, I helped to found the College of Art Theatre Group. In my First Year I had joined the Edinburgh University Dramatic Society, taking a small part in *Othello* and a number of parts in the first amateur production put on during the Edinburgh Festival – *Peer Gynt*. The College of Art Theatre Group was for me more exciting. The main producer was a gifted member of staff in the School of Painting, Alan Carr. I became chairman of the Group and usually assistant producer. My neighbour in the architectural studio was at one time John Arden. When he said he had written a play, we put it on; he gave up architecture and became a celebrated playwright.

The city of Edinburgh, I recognised, was for me not just a place to study; it was a work of art, a civilisation, an education in itself. For me, again, the major influences at the College of Art were probably not the teachers or even my fellow students; they were the artists and writers and performers. I continued to spend my days sketching in Edinburgh. I attended concerts and plays. It was not until I went to Edinburgh that I attended a symphony concert for the first time. It was a performance by the Berlin Philharmonic Orchestra and their concluding number was Tchaikovsky's *Fourth Symphony*, conducted by Sergiu Cellibidache. It was an overwhelming experience.

Being very poor, I was nevertheless determined to go to as many as possible of the orchestral concerts in the Usher Hall. Standing penniless one evening outside the gallery door, I noticed that there were a few moments between the attendant closing the box office and locking the front door when I could slip through and up the staircase without being seen. I therefore attended orchestral concerts (with the exception of a few bars of the overture) for several years until I was caught.

But I had chosen the College in Edinburgh so that I could study art as well as architecture. I began to study it in a very practical way. Willie Wilson was a painter and a very good stained-glass artist. A fellow student took me to see him. He knew my father's work and admired it. He took me out sketching. I learned more from him in a few afternoons sketching than I did from most of the classes in the College. His approach to a landscape or a group of buildings became mine and still shapes my own paintings. He was endlessly generous and hospitable. For many years I called in regularly at his studio and house.

His story was eventually a sad one; he contracted diabetes, tried to run his studio despite that, became blind and eventually left Edinburgh and went south to stay with his sister. I tried to contact him but failed; I had lost touch with him, to my lasting regret. I still have the paintings that, with haphazard generosity, he gave me.

There were other, very different, encounters. Within a few weeks of arriving in Edinburgh I met a school acquaintance, older than myself, who had been in the army and had now come to Edinburgh to study English literature. Bruce Cooper was a Yorkshireman, from Pocklington in the East Riding. To some extent, he took me over. He persuaded me to leave the admirable lodgings I had found and join him in 'digs' in another part of the city. We shared a study-bedroom. He persuaded me to draw posters for various university societies, including the Poetry Society. The workload for architectural students being a heavy one, I made most of these drawings for posters in the middle of the night. He became increasingly irritated at being kept awake. One morning, he left early. In the post that arrived that morning I received a letter from him requesting me to leave immediately. I apologised to the landlord, took my rucksack and walked off down the road, looking for somewhere to stay, and was accosted by a fat little man who wanted me to come with him to the Turkish baths. I refused. But perhaps it was a warning. It was the start of many moves around Edinburgh, and some even more embarrassing experiences.

But despite Bruce's despicable behaviour, we remained friends. Later in our student years we travelled together to Ireland, hitchhiking at first and then putting what money we had together and hiring a wretched little car in Cork in which we drove along the west coast. Not having a tent, we slept (in the inevitable rain) under any trees we could find. That was in graveyards. We wedged ourselves between graves and kept as warm as we could. Often we woke in the morning to see a row of faces peering over the wall and always got treated to breakfast.

Among the places we visited were Cistercian and Benedictine monasteries. The most spectacular were Mount Melleray (of which I made a painting) and the Benedictine Abbey at Glenstal. Towards the end of our irresponsible holiday, we drove up to the Cistercian abbey at Roscrea and stopped in front of the abbey when the car ran out of petrol. We had no money to buy more.

The Prior at the time was a well-known monk and psychiatrist, Fr Eugene Boylan. As we talked to him one evening about our attitude to Christianity, he became concerned and eventually asked me what it was that was worrying me. I had to tell him that it was not theology or faith but the fact that we had no money. He went back to his room, pulled out some money from under the mattress and lent it to us on the condition that we gave it back to his mother. He told us that he always kept money that he could lend to penitents in the confessional whom he recognised did not need his prayers as much as his psychiatric help. Our need was more mundane but possibly more urgent!

After leaving Edinburgh University, Bruce Cooper went to Cambridge to train as a teacher and taught first in schools and then in a college of further education in the north of England before leaving for Northern Ireland where he became Dean of Management Studies at Ulster Polytechnic and organised courses for both the police and the 'peace

The King's Manor, University of York

The graveyard, Little Hampden, Bucks

'Nativity' stained glass panel by J.E. Nuttgens

Blue Dawn at Claydon Lock, Oxford Canal

York

Leeds Town Hall

Fairfax House, York

people' in the midst of the 'troubles'. He died of a heart attack at the age of fifty-two. Senior officials of both the polytechnic and the police attended his funeral at Pocklington.

Student life in Edinburgh was not so isolated but part of the city. Early in my university career I joined two other students in renting a flat. One was the architectural student, a keen Quaker, with whom I drove to Italy. The other, Gerry Watts, was a Catholic who had been at Downside and was studying brewing at the Heriot-Watt Technical College. When he left, after a year, his place was taken by Bill Culican, a quite brilliant student of archaeology. Gerry Watts married Biddy's best friend; Bill Culican married Biddy's sister. I suppose it was the most effective marriage agency we could have devised.

And I married Biddy, Dr Badenoch's second daughter. Mainly because of the length of my course, and because we shared the Catholic faith and respected its teaching about marriage and birth control, we could neither live together nor get married for many years. We were engaged for four of them, during which I learned a lot from Biddy and respected her unshakeable convictions. I also took out classes in the University, notably in English literature, where I could sit beside her and learn about literature from her.

And that leads me to describe the originality of the course of study which I decided to join. The College of Art had already set up, in conjunction with the University, a degree in Fine Art, whereby students studied drawing and painting or sculpture in the College for the whole of the course and took out various subjects in the University to enable them to obtain both a College diploma and an MA (Hons) in the University.

During my first year, the College authorities decided to develop the same course in architecture. Five of us were persuaded to try it out. Ironically, having rejected a university education and entered a College of Art, I was now accepted by a university. I joined it enthusiastically. I thought it might give me the intellectual stimulation that I was missing – and even show me what modern architecture was all about! Of that first group, I was the only one to survive; then another four staggered through before the course was abolished. I obtained a first-class honours degree – which means that I have a unique degree which can never be taken again. It did not make me a better architect.

I was not excused from any parts of the architecture course. In addition to that course, in successive years, I took out university classes in the History of Art, English Literature, Moral Philosophy and then Aesthetics and wrote a final dissertation on an architectural historical subject. The course was absurdly packed. But it was not the variety of subjects that made it difficult, it was transferring from an art college studio to a university lecture hall, walking hurriedly along the road between the College and the University and trying to adjust my mind. (Having a caliper on one leg which squeaked as I walked, dogs followed me and snapped at my ankles). It was a drastic change from the art of doing and making to the discipline of listening and thinking.

The first Professor of Architecture in Edinburgh did not resolve anything. Gordon Brown had been a paratrooper during the war and then became Deputy Head of the Architectural Association School in London. He was a tall, bald man who wore a long white smock and radiated self-confidence. I thought him inspirational; he was, in fact, totally irresponsible. After he had taken out a dozen or more bank accounts on the strength of the same university salary and overdrawn them all, he was persuaded to leave. He went to Hong Kong, where he lasted for a few years and, having appointed three people to one job, departed quickly for Salt Lake City. He returned to London after another series of blunders and died there – miserably, I was told. But his crazy career had a lasting effect on mine.

The chaos in direction and staffing meant that not only was I taking a new and unusual course but there was no one to supervise it. My Director of Studies was a delightful university lecturer in mediaeval history, later to become the

Professor. He would look up anxiously when I came into his room at the start of an academic year, groan loudly and agree to sign any documentation if I undertook not to come and see him again for at least another year. On that basis – with only one mistake – I steered myself through that complicated and confusing course.

The College of Art staff showed no interest in it whatsoever. One year, as a result of some administrative confusion over the length of the course, I transferred to the School of Drawing and Painting and enjoyed myself enormously painting in the College whilst studying aesthetics in the University. The fine art studio for drawing and painting was very different from the architectural studio. That was essentially serious but had its lighter moments when (led by Sandy Brown, the jazz-band leader and later acoustical consultant to the BBC) we made music by playing pipes, beating and scraping on T-squares and set squares and tin trunks. The drawing and painting studio was hot and sweaty and sometimes full of song. One girl sang all the way through Beethoven symphonies. It also had its lighter moments, when, for example, the naked model Vera was so infuriated by a mature student, Major Chambers Crabtree, whom she thought had insulted her, that she leaped off the rostrum and pursued him round the Sculpture Court – a stout figure in a kilt pursued by a naked monster howling for vengeance. I later lost all my life paintings. My brother Joe painted over one of them; the others, including one of an out-of-work actor called Sean Connery, were left in a cottage we occupied on the Moray Firth and (I hope and doubt) may have given a few moments' pleasure to the local fishermen.

There was at least one other disaster caused by the irresponsible first Professor. He abolished the teaching of architectural history because he thought it irrelevant to the modern movement in architecture. As a result, I have never studied the history of architecture in any detail but merely written about it. I acquired my knowledge of architectural history in the College library and the public library. Among many other studies, I found there Niklaus Pevsner's *Pioneers of the Modern Movement* (later republished as *Pioneers of Modern Design*) and in a state of euphoria decided that at last I knew what modern architecture was about. It was a logical social movement, spanning the years of change from William Morris to Walter Gropius!

Whatever the intellectual confusion, I had been making drawings all the time. A few weeks before the end of my Third Year, it was realised by the staff of the college (the Professor having by that time been persuaded to depart) that in order to satisfy professional demands, we must have some remarks for history. The long-suffering Acting Head recruited a retired city architect who spent a fortnight giving us lectures about the history of architecture in Edinburgh, and we prepared sheets of study of selected periods. I produced studies of Edinburgh buildings from the Middle Ages and the nineteenth century and was awarded an outstanding mark. Though I really wanted to be a great designer, it seemed my course was being set in a different direction.

The effect on me of this chaotic and ill-devised education was not to learn more about architecture but to get to know more about the organisation of both a university and a college. Because of the oddity of my course – and because within a year or two I was the only person taking it – I got to know many of the senior university administrators. For example, the Secretary of the University (who in England would be described as the Registrar) was Charles Stewart, a most ingenious and subtle man. He told me later that he only knew one student a year, and in that particular year I was the student. The Principal and Vice-Chancellor, Sir Edward Appleton, had made his name during the war as the discoverer of whatever in the stratosphere made possible 'radar'. I drew out some diagrams for him so that he could explain radar to the Duke of Edinburgh.

I began to feel important and confident. Appleton and Stewart called me in one day to discuss a crucial problem. That was the need for a new Professor of Architecture. The fact was, they said, that there was no one else to consult – I was the only person who understood the course.

Meantime, I had some success in the University, not so much in architectural design but in other areas. Having taken English literature and attended classes among some 300 other students, I won the class medal. I remember the look of astonishment on the face of the Professor of English when he discovered who had won the medal; for I had always been late for lectures, having walked from the College of Art. As I limped through the lecture room, the students followed an old Scottish tradition of stamping in time with my footsteps and thus interrupting the lecture. They stamped again when I limped up for my medal.

I also took an active part in one of the Rectorial elections. The students of the Scottish universities (whose constitutions are based not on mediaeval Paris but on mediaeval Bologna), elect every few years a Rector who becomes chairman of the University Court. He rarely chairs it but leaves it to an 'assessor' appointed by him. He is usually a man or woman of some distinction – a tradition that died a few years later when the students elected another student. The first student so elected, another Gordon Brown, is now (as I write) Chancellor of the Exchequer.

But in my time, a group was formed with a view to the election of Evelyn Waugh. My job was publicity. Needless to say, the majority of students had never heard of him, especially the medical students (who duly elected Sir Alexander Fleming, the discoverer of penicillin). But our campaign was brilliant and recognised as such. Evelyn Waugh's novels were being published by Penguin. We designed the cover for a new Penguin book entitled *The Rector* by Evelyn Waugh. On one occasion I was knocked unconsciousness by rival students armed with hockey sticks. Someone sent a photograph of my bruised head to Evelyn Waugh, who replied that he was glad we were supporting him forcefully.

But the most influential figure in my Edinburgh education was in neither the University nor the College; one of the strengths of a great university city is that it contains so

From *Burke Street* by George Scott-Moncrieff

many literary and artistic personalities. Some time in the early 1950s I had become involved in the formation and running of the University's Fine Art Society, which organised exhibitions of contemporary art. At the opening of one of these exhibitions in the Upper Library Hall of the University of Edinburgh, I was introduced to George Scott-Moncrieff. He had just taken a bite out of a meringue. He said something welcoming which I failed to catch; whatever it was, the meringue burst into fragments all over me. By the time he had removed all the bits and wiped me down, we had become friends. It was the most valuable friendship I ever made.

I had read his Batsford book on *Edinburgh* and was familiar with his opinions. He was a convert to Roman Catholicism and had the utmost contempt for the Church of Scotland; but he knew Edinburgh at first hand and had explored nearly all its roads and alleyways and all the closes and wynds that I had sketched. He himself lived in a remarkable flat in James Court near the top of the Royal Mile. It was an early eighteenth-century building and the flat was three floors up on one side and eight on the other because of the slope of the hill. It was the tenement beside the one where Boswell had entertained Dr Johnson in the eighteenth century and the very flat in which Patrick Geddes had written *Cities of Evolution* at the start of the twentieth century.

A little man just inside the door embossed letter headings, a journalist tried to write books further along the passage, and at one stage, a Judge from the High Court installed a grand piano and came in to play Beethoven's sonatas between court cases. George's room looked out across Princes Street. On a good day you could see over the Forth to Fife and even as far as Ben Lomond. We spent many evenings sitting beside the window drinking coffee (which he ground from beans in a wonderfully old-fashioned grinder), talking endlessly about the meaning of life. He was a convinced Catholic, who said he never got over his wonder at the Real Presence during the consecration. I used to accompany him to Mass.

His own story was remarkable. He had a harelip and a cleft palette, disguising the former with a scruffy moustache but never quite able to conquer the latter. But when you knew him and had learned to understand everything he said, you found he was the most hilarious conversationalist. He was so funny that, at times, I could hardly stand. He was generally known as 'Scomo' and had innumerable friends. In his younger days, before the Second World War, he had written a number of very promising novels and married a brilliant girl, Ann, who was herself a superb story-teller and poet. She bore him three children (two boys and a girl). Suffering from a depression following a miscarriage, living on the edge of the sea at Nairn, she walked out of the house one morning and into the sea (as far as anyone could tell). She was never seen again and her body was never found. Edwin Muir wrote a brief and very moving poem about her. George looked after the three children. He rented a cottage on the Isle of Eigg and there wrote a novel, *Death's Bright Shadow*, in which he tried to sort out his confusion and despair about her death. It tells a great deal about him and her; but more than that, it contains important and unusual perceptions.

I remember one evening sitting beside the window in James Court when somehow the conversation moved round to the subject of happiness. I was myself unhappy at the time and asked him if he had a good definition of happiness. 'No,' he said. 'I regret that I have not. But I do have a good definition of unhappiness. Unhappiness is the refusal to suffer.' He was, I think, in that sense, the happiest man I had ever met.

I suppose I contributed a certain amount to him. I acted in one of his plays, illustrated one of his books and produced some massive lettering for a banner for his play *Fotheringhay* which was performed during an Edinburgh Festival. I even found him quotes – from Dostoievski, for example. Here are two of them: 'In abstract love of humanity, one almost only loves oneself' and 'There are always a certain kind of people who, having found a little trace of humanitarianism in their hearts, think that no one has ever thought like them before and that they must be in the avant-garde of civilisation'.

But I gained infinitely more from George than I ever gave to him. He made very little money from his books or plays and lived mainly by writing reviews of plays and exhibitions. I went with him to plays in Edinburgh and exhibitions in many places. They were often hilarious occasions. When he spent a year in America, he lent me his room in James Court and his job as a reviewer. I learned to be a journalist and to type, writing reviews late at night and sending them through to the newspaper in Glasgow.

The visitors to James Court were just as remarkable as George, some so eccentric as to seem dotty. One of the most memorable was Major Sleigh. The Major was small, wiry and incredibly poor. He carried his belongings on various bootlaces round his neck – his watch on one end and his keys on the other, resting in his waistcoat pockets. He had been in the Boer War, the Great War and almost any war you could think of. I once watched him having a bath in a tub in front of the fire in the little house he occupied; he was covered in scars. He insisted that George was the most delightful man he knew – 'Dear Scomo,' he would say in a singsong voice, 'he really is the most wonderful man.'

George was very fond of him. The Major combined what seemed to me two fundamentally irreconcilable points of view. He was a Scottish Nationalist and an enthusiast for the League of Empire Loyalists. He had no time for what he called 'the white Jews of Whitehall'. On Sunday afternoons, he mounted a soapbox and spoke at the Mound (the Edinburgh equivalent of Hyde Park Corner). I heard him one afternoon explaining why the blacks should never be allowed to run their countries: 'They have only just come down from the trees.' So apprehensive was I when an enormous black man strode up to him, that I hurriedly stood beside him in the faint hope of saving his life. The black man shook the major by the hand and said, 'Major, you dead right.' The Major lived for a time in a small flat in Charles Street and ended in the nursing home that had formerly been a pauper's hospital in Queensberry House at the foot of the Royal Mile.

Another close friend of George's was Hew Lorimer, son of the great Scottish architect, Robert Lorimer, and himself a celebrated sculptor. Hew lived in Kellie Castle in Fife, a dramatic Scottish castle or effectively fortified manor of the fifteenth to seventeenth centuries. I remember one of the most hilarious weekends I ever spent when I drove George to Kellie. We could hardly stop laughing even when we went to church (the Catholic church, of course) on Sunday morning.

Some years later, in the early 1960s, George decided to get married again. He had met a beautiful girl who was a student at the University, ocupying a flat near James Court. He was fifty-three; she was twenty-three. I took them away on their honeymoon, left them in the Borders and drove on to York, which is another part of my story. Eileen bore him four boys before he died of a heart attack. His eldest son (from his previous marriage) was approximately the same age as Eileen. She married him and they had a daughter. But that is also another story.

My memories of George are of a wonderfully critical person who combined a scathing wit with endless kindness. It was the first time I had got to know a professional writer – that is, someone writing every day. He was fussy about personal foibles, most unfussy about his own comfort. I remember one occasion when he was about to go to Italy and walked down the Royal Mile to a cheap shop which sold, he said, excellent second-hand trousers. He came back with a pair of trousers with a hole in the leg so I sent him back. He returned with a much longer pair whose legs we had to roll up and pin.

Living in the tenement building in James Court, which was entered from the Lawnmarket at the top of the Royal

Mile, I became obsessed with the place. The flat was decrepit and possibly (some people thought) dangerous. It had a WC but no bath. George had fitted up a camper's shower, where you stood in a zinc tub and pulled a string to release water over your head. That was (relatively) modern. The rest of the dwelling had been battered into shape by several hundred years of variegated history. It was at its busiest and most crowded in the nineteenth century.

George introduced me to two books that gave a unique insight into the life of the Old Town at that time. James M'Levy was a detective who had emigrated from Ireland at the age of seventeen and became a Scottish detective in 1833. In just over thirty years he chalked up no less than 2,220 cases and in his retirement wrote two books: *Curiosities of Crime in Edinburgh* and *The Sliding Scale of Life*, which he described as 'Thirty years' observations of falling men and women in Edinburgh'.

He knew all the closes and wynds and the tall tenements that are known in Edinburgh as 'lands'. Of two such lands in Leith Wynd, he described the 'Happy Land' as 'divided into numerous dens, inhabited by thieves, robbers, thimblers, pickpockets, abandoned women, drunken destitutes and here and there chance-begotten brats, squatting with hunger or lying dead for days after they should have been buried'. Nearby was the 'Holy Land', given over to 'prostitution, with its accompaniment intoxication'. He described himself and the inhabitants of the 'lands' as old friends: 'The Happy Land is a great conglomeration of *stews* . . . all the people who inhabit this accumulation of dens understand each other. It is a world by itself, with no law ruling except force, no compunction except fear, no religion except that of the devil . . . to them it is perfectly natural.'

I began to know – and meet – these ghostly characters. Some of the present day's characters seemed direct descendants, like my friend Jimmy Miller. Tall, hideously haggard and reeking of cheap spirits, when looking at prosperous people, he sometimes became apocalyptic, shaking his bony hand and shouting, 'God will come and strike them doon!' And little Mr Campbell, red-faced in a mustard-coloured overcoat bulging with belongings that he wouldn't leave in his doss-house because, he said, the people there would steal them. The whole place, especially after my long conversations with George Scott-Moncrieff, had, I began to think, adopted me as one of its denizens. When Mr Miller asked me for money one day to buy some shoes, I showed him the sole of one of mine; he offered to lend me some money.

That was my life in James Court. I recognised it bit by bit as a special experience of 'tenement living'. The tenements in Edinburgh (and later those in Glasgow) are a peculiarly Scottish solution to the problem of housing as many people as possible on a restricted site, often on a slope and close together to keep warm. As they grew, mostly after the seventeenth century, they housed many social groups: tradesmen on the ground floor, aristocracy on the main floor (the first floor), professional people a little higher, the poor at the top. Even in the formal eighteenth-century Georgian New Town, some of the apparently unified houses were (and are) tenements.

My own lodgings varied from comfortable to squalid and comfortable again. After Bruce Cooper expelled me from our 'digs' I spent some months in a Catholic hostel, Aquinas House, and a year in a comfortable basement flat in the New Town which I shared with Dave Barnes and his divorced mother. Later I moved to George Square.

We already knew George Square. The Badenochs lived there and so did many university professors. It was the first development to the south of the old city, with coherent but not identical stone houses on four sides of a four-acre communal garden. What later destroyed it was the University's decision to expand. The Old College on the South Bridge (designed by Robert Adam) was on a cramped site and surrounded by inferior buildings. But they were not readily available for replacement. It was much easier for the University to acquire houses in George Square, demolish most of them (leaving only the west side) and create a new campus with modern buildings. I found myself in an embarrassingly ambivalent position, working in the Square for the architect of the new buildings and at the same time briefing the objectors and writing manifestos. I had already represented the Georgian Society at a public enquiry about the replacement of a crescent in the New Town; I now became even more involved in the growing movement of what later was described as 'conservation'. And I began to see the university in a new light – not just a civilised centre for the dispassionate pursuit of learning but a big business with a developed capacity for arrogance and ruthlessness.

This varied and sometimes hectic life was, I now recognise, as much a part of my education as any of the lectures and tutorials in college or university. That must be the case for any student – learning to live and love in the streets as well as the lecture room and library. It may be that Edinburgh was special. It was unlike any other place I had known and seemed to offer a special attitude to the world – what an Edinburgh historian later described as 'the democratic intellect'. Whether it was the city or the country or the influence of writers and artists, or maybe all of them, I found myself, almost as I had in hospital, determined that I would never try to live at a higher level than everyone else and certainly not more than I could afford. If I could only afford to live in a slum, I would do so – as I shall describe later in this chapter.

But let me return to student life. In the University I took part in regular debates run by the Dialectic Society. In the College I was more and more involved in acting and singing and drawing – and always organising. I began to understand modern architecture and design buildings which might not be entirely modern but were eclectic, descendants (I thought) of the early modern movement and the turn of the century.

In my final year as an architectural student, the situation was drastically changed by the arrival of a new Professor. That was Robert Matthew, who had been a student at the College of Art School of Architecture, had joined the

Department of Health for Scotland and become its chief architect and then become Architect to the London County Council. He was there in time for the Festival of Britain in 1951 and seized the chance to put the architects' department of London County Council in the forefront of international architectural design. On holiday in the Shetlands, he told me, he received a telegram asking if it would be possible to design and build a concert hall in time for the Festival. He replied instantly that it was and that moreover his department would design it. The Royal Festival Hall is the result – a superb product by architects and engineers and builders and scientists and (of course) musicians.

In those post-war years, however, the major demand was not for cultural buildings but for housing – the satisfaction of a huge post-war housing demand. London County Council was responsible for a major programme of local authority housing. Matthew was a protagonist of what came to be known as 'social architecture'. The programme was huge. As the quickest way to meet the demand, the first tower blocks were erected, a mistake which was not recognised for many years. For the time being, English social housing was celebrated internationally.

Matthew arrived in a little car in Edinburgh, supervised the work of some of the final year students (including me) and began to build up his own architectural practice. He recruited two of my contemporaries to work in his office and later recruited me to help set up a new university department. The office grew rapidly and, at one stage, had almost 1,000 members. His first partner was Stirrat Johnson-Marshall who had been the chief architect in the government's Department of Education. With Matthew's background in housing and Johnson-Marshall's background in schools, they had a formidable expertise. The practice expanded at an astonishing rate.

Meantime, Matthew had changed my life. I produced a thesis design for a Blackfriars monastery for Edinburgh which was not so much a brilliant feat of imagination as a workable project resulting from a thorough and scholarly dissertation. The result was both a diploma from the College of Art and a first-class honours MA from the University. I received a number of postgraduate grants which would enable me to carry out research. That is the start of another story.

On returning to Edinburgh as Professor of Architecture, Robert Matthew had decided that it would be beneficial both to the country and to architecture if serious studies were made into Scottish native architecture. He was an exponent of social architecture, the architecture of the common man and woman. It seemed to him – and remains today – a critical failure of the international modern style that it seemed unable to accommodate regional variations of a serious architectural kind. If, therefore, studies were made of the vernacular architecture of the various regions of Scotland, it might be possible to analyse its roots and discover a Scottish architecture which would be realistic, recognisable and popular with its users.

He himself could give an example. Soon involved with the Hydroelectric Board, he rejected the pompous traditional buildings that the Board had previously commissioned and designed power stations for Lochay and Cashlie which, in contrast to the rather stuffy buildings that the Board had so far erected, were an exercise in what looked to me a very possible Scottish modern architecture. They had random rubble stone walling, large window embrasures and a low-pitched green copper roof. He took me to see and discuss the new building at Lochay.

I was impressed. He asked me to assemble a bibliography of Scottish architecture which I started shortly after graduation. As his only postgraduate student interested in Scottish architecture, he suggested that I make a regional survey of the vernacular architecture of the north-east Lowlands of Scotland: Aberdeenshire, Banffshire, Moray and Nairn, and, to give me a base from which to operate, arranged for me to be attached to the School of Scottish Studies in the University of Edinburgh.

It changed my life. The School of Scottish Studies was

(and probably still is) a confused and confusing research centre. The main occupation of its members was the collection, recording and publication of Scottish folklore and folk songs. I shared a room with a social anthropologist who was collecting information about 'material culture' – ordinary everyday things used by and in traditional communities. That connected with vernacular architecture, which is the architecture of everyday people, not usually designed by architects but built by local communities.

At this point I must try to explain – and possibly understand – the man who came to dominate and shape my professional life. Robert Hogg Matthew was an enigma. Thoroughly Scottish in appearance and speech, he became an international figure, unpretentious, softly spoken but giving an irresistible impression of competence and natural authority. What was his message? In one of the rare seminars he gave to his students at Edinburgh University he said quietly in answer to a question: 'The job of an architect is solving other people's problems.'

That was much more important than it may at first sound. Other people's problems, not the architect's own. He did not, unlike most architects, talk about himself. He was a puzzling and sometimes infuriating figure. He casually dominated people and institutions, relatives and colleagues, but never in a forceful or aggressive way. He just seemed to be in charge; if he chaired a meeting it took shape and without any hurry finished on time.

A senior university colleague once asked me if Matthew was as stupid as he seemed. I said that it would be a serious mistake to take it for granted. I once collected many of the doodles he made on his blotting pad and asked a perceptive behavioural psychologist in the University to interpret them. He failed. 'They tell me only,' he said, 'that he is a very private person.'

But I did become familiar with his own architectural designs and began to recognise their characteristics. Before the firm expanded and worked in many parts of the world, he produced the initial designs for Turnhouse Airport (now

70

demolished), the hydroelectric power stations, Crombie Hall in the University of Aberdeen, the Arts Tower in Dundee University and New Zealand House in Haymarket, London. They were simple in outline and careful in their choice of materials. Above all, they revealed his understanding of three-dimensional space as the very essence of architecture.

In the University, the School of Scottish Studies was riddled with internal dissension. The Scots have always fought each other as much as the 'foreigners'; here it seemed that all the specialists hated each other. My companion was an expert at stirring up hatred, with occasional 'round robins'. As a few years went by, I found myself increasingly the recipient of woeful stories.

But the exploration of the north-east of Scotland and the discovery of its vernacular buildings was a constant delight. Matthew's contribution as my supervisor was to give me the name of a former colleague and friend at Aberdeen University who might be helpful; for with the expansion of his architectural practice, Matthew had become too busy to supervise my studies. I met him on one occasion at Craigievar Castle, where he was working in an attic as the guest of Lord Sempill. As far as I remember, we did not discuss my studies but looked at his designs for New Zealand House in London.

But at Aberdeen University, I met another postgraduate of my age who had made a study of economic developments in the same region. He was unreservedly helpful and gave me all the crucial references I needed. With that as a background – and having bought for £40 a somewhat derelict little Ford car – I explored the four counties and visited every village. I arranged to work in two estate offices, studying the plans of farm buildings and the planned villages, as well as roads, rivers and harbours.

The fact is that the whole region was transformed between the middle of the seventeenth century and the end of the nineteenth century. That transformation involved the enclosure of open land, the destruction of old 'farm towns', the building of new planned villages, the introduction of new crops and the building of new big farms. Some areas developed native industries. In Banffshire, for example, there were founded during that period no less than 27 distilleries. I visited most of them.

But visually the most exciting area of my study was the group of fishing villages which stretched northwards from Aberdeen, round the corner ('the cold shoulder of Buchan') and along the Moray Firth as far as Nairn and Inverness. I photographed these vivid colourful houses, formerly painted annually during the winter when fishing was too dangerous. The colours are vivid; their patterns varied from the black and white of Portnockie to the green and scarlet of Portgordon.

The fisher folk are very private, especially if they are Brethren (open or closed) worshipping and singing in the upper rooms that constitute their chapels where 'the word of God is preached on Sundays'. I met many of them but visited few of their houses. On the other hand, I called on Peter Anson who lived in a fisher house in Macduff and was a brilliant draughtsman, drawing fisher boats and writing books on fisher boats and fisher folk. My father had met him at Eric Gill's house and insisted that I must introduce myself. It was a memorable experience. He had been a monk and later published a fascinating illustrated book on *Fashions in Church Furnishing*. I stayed with him, visited abbeys and monasteries and churches and learned a lot about churches of all denominations.

Meantime, shortly after graduation, Biddy Badenoch and I had been married at the Dominican Chapel in George Square, Edinburgh. For our honeymoon, George Scot-Moncrieff lent us his cottage on the Isle of Eigg. That in itself was a new experience, sailing from Mallaig and living in a small cottage, now demolished, learning about the Highlands and Islands, appreciating the Gaelic language, joining in 'ceilidhs' and exploring the hills and dales. And always making drawings, some of which must still be there. It was

Visit to Amersfoort, Holland, 1955

Valke Straat, looking to the Muurhuizen

Door to No 227
MUURHUIZEN

a suitably poverty-stricken and unpretentious introduction to married life.

When we returned to Edinburgh, in fulfilment of my principles, we did not look for a respectable house; we bought, for £150, a tenement flat in Buccleuch Street. It consisted of two rooms – what in Scotland is known as a 'room and kitchen' or sometimes a 'single end'. It was on the first floor of a four-storey tenement built in 1727 and close to the University. It had no bathroom or lavatory. There was a toilet on the corner of the tenement stair, shared by all the inhabitants, and we had a cold tap in the kitchen. We kept it for three years during which we occasionally let it and eventually sold it to the University for £200. That seemed a handsome profit. A few years later, the University amalgamated it with some other rooms on that floor and sold the lot for £34,000. But for us it was the right place to start our married life. My postgraduate grants were quite inadequate to support a family. So, soon after returning to Edinburgh from the north-east Lowlands, I started writing articles, reviews and criticisms – anything to make a little money.

For a time, while exploring the four counties, we lived in the north-east. It was a rare experience. The Catholic Bishop of Aberdeen, Francis Walsh, shared – like Lord Sempill – Dr Badenoch's devotion to compost. We had met him in the Badenoch's house. He leased us an empty house on the edge of the Moray Firth at Portessie just east of Buckie. We moved there with our first son, and from there toured the whole region. That also was a rare experience. One afternoon I arrived in my little car at a village in Aberdeenshire, at that time inhabited by tinkers. Having gone into a house and tapped out an elementary tune on the piano, I was quickly surrounded by people with violins, accordians and mouth organs. Suddenly I found myself in the midst of an impromptu musical party.

Although I was in due course awarded a Doctorate of Philosophy for my study of the *Architecture and Settlements of the North-East Lowlands of Scotland*, I cannot pretend that I made any contribution to the development of a national Scottish architecture. I had listed and described the natural materials: stone, timber, plaster, various types of wall and roof; I had drawn out the plans of villages and houses; more significantly, I had tried to discover why the fisher folk painted their houses in the most vivid colours. But I had failed to identify any components that could be the basis for a true modern Scottish vernacular. In any case I did not know enough about architectural practice. And my supervisor, Professor Matthew, had become totally immersed in a growing architectural practice as well as the day-to-day problems of a university department. That requires a special explanation.

Shortly after my last year in the School of Architecture, Matthew had walked out of the College of Art after a serious disagreement with the Principal and persuaded the University to let him set up a separate Department of Architecture. It was, I thought, absurd to have two schools of architecture in one city; but it was not unknown elsewhere. The University allocated part of an eighteenth-century house in George Square and Robert Matthew set about the foundation of a new department. To whom could he look for relevant experience and knowledge of university politics? I was the only person in Edinburgh with a university degree in architecture. Matthew himself did not have a degree. I soon learned how to devise ordinances and regulations and carried out all sorts of administrative tasks for the Professor.

The MA degree which I had taken was abolished and a new degree – Bachelor of Architecture – was established. At first that was conducted in both the University and the College. The students of architecture were enrolled in both the University and the College of Art, spent their first three years in the College whilst attending a weekly seminar in the University and then transferred for their final two years to the University. My job, apart from administering the course, was organising and teaching in those seminars. It did seem to me that the students would have benefited if I had had more practical experience. I had obtained my professional qualification with the minimum of office experience, carried out a few architectural jobs and concentrated on teaching and research.

It was obvious that the new department needed experienced academic staff. Matthew recruited three senior lecturers with whom he had worked in practice. Percy Johnson-Marshall, brother of Matthew's partner Stirrat, had been a colleague at the LCC in London and came to Edinburgh to be in charge of town planning; Frank Clark, who had worked on the landscape for the Festival of Britain, was put in charge of landscape design; Eric Stevenson, who was an architect in the Department of Health for Scotland, came in to head a new research unit set up by Matthew, with money from the Ford Foundation, to enquire into housing. We planned and started a new degree which was eventually a full-time five-year degree. Matthew's interests and experience were central to the whole approach, including the setting up of the Housing Research Unit. We were concerned with social architecture, especially housing and towns. Matthew's architectural practice expanded in those very fields at the same time as the University was developing the new courses of study.

Looking back on it now, I am astonished at the freedom I was given to plan a course *de novo*. Such a privilege was not, unfortunately, obvious to me at the time. Such planning requires maturity. At the time I was embarrassed by the fact that there appeared to be no guidelines, no rules, nothing to tell us what we ought to be doing. And since I myself was singularly short of practical experience in architecture, I found myself thrown back on talking, reading and constantly picking other people's brains, hoping all the time to find a rationale as the basis for a course.

It was clear to me from the start that architecture in the University was not among the reputable subjects that a university usually taught. Architecture, after all, had been taught in a College of Art. Rumour had it that the Professor of English had remarked at the Senate that if the University

76

were going to teach architecture, it would be teaching plumbing next. In fact, as the Professor of Architecture later remarked, it does now teach plumbing, but calls it 'Building Science'.

It occurred to me, being one of the few university graduates in architecture in Scotland, and having been fascinated by my studies in English and in philosophy, that I might turn my mind to proving how respectable an academic discipline architecture was. I therefore carried out a study of architectural education, and, after many discussions and arguments, produced my own analysis of architecture in terms of academic categories. Architecture depended, I thought, on four basic academic disciplines: science, philosophy, art and design.

Design was what we specifically had to offer. All the other disciplines were disciplines studied better and to a higher level in other departments of the University. Design was something of our own. It was therefore essential, it seemed to me, to insist that design was an activity every bit as formidable and as fundamental as the discipline of science. The problem was, of course, to know exactly what was meant by design. It was an even greater problem in university terms to say how design could function like a university discipline, the main characteristics of most of which were the accumulation of facts, criticism and understanding, and the pursuit of the subject no matter where it might lead.

Our discipline – design – was essentially creative and practical. It often depended upon inadequate information, required all sorts of snap judgements, and had to be completed in order to exist at all. It consumed very long hours, it might not be verbal, and our best students might not be particularly articulate. Nevertheless, the pursuit of academic disciplines must be the very essence of academic study and research.

Because of the nature of architecture there has always been a tension between academic learning and practical experience. I myself was short of experience; some of my colleagues had plenty of it, but were short of academic maturity. Hoping to bring the whole thing together, the Professor had obtained money from a foundation and set up a research project into housing. We would thus be academically respectable. But that led to fantastic disruption inside the department, which affected my attitude towards the department and ultimately towards research. Even while the department was small it became clear to me that there was a constant tension between the activity of teaching and the need to do research. My own fascination was not really with research but with teaching.

Taking a summer off I completed a thesis and obtained the Ph.D. But the most exciting part of my work was teaching students, particularly senior students – not only teaching them architectural design, but engaging in seminars and discussions with people from other disciplines, trying between us to discover an education which would stand us all in good stead no matter what in the end we might do. I stood somewhere on a threshold between the activities of making, designing, drawing, thinking and creating, and the disciplines of philosophy, history, science and art.

Biddy and I had moved from our little room and kitchen in Buccleuch Street to a more spacious university flat in Buccleuch Place and then to a delightful two-storey flat at the top of a Georgian building in George Square. We had three more children.

By this time I had become more and more deeply involved in architecture, partly as a practitioner, more as a teacher and writer, contributing regularly, for example, to the *Weekly Scotsman*. I was busiest in Matthew's university department – a role he later described as his Departmental Registrar.

I had already built a bell-tower onto the Catholic church at Mallaig in the Western Highlands. The parish priest at Morar, Canon McNeil, insisted that no slates should be dislodged from the roof (it had taken many years, he said, to make it waterproof on its exposed site near the sea). But he had a fine bell and wanted to hear it ringing. I designed a free-standing tower linked to the church. To supervise the work I caught the 4.10 a.m. train from Edinburgh to Glasgow and then took the West Highland line over Rannoch Moor to Fort William and thence Mallaig. The builder, Alexander Grieve, was shrewd and cunning and kept me in my place with a sardonic wit. I produced designs for a new convent for an enclosed order of Dominican nuns in Glasgow which was never built (they had no money).

To my surprise – and ultimately to my delight – I was invited to join the Catholic cathedral choir. It was not the usual society of volunteers; it had just recruited a brilliant composer and choirmaster, Arthur Oldham, who after being a pupil and performer for Benjamin Britten, had come to Edinburgh to recover from a serious breakdown. He transformed the singing, guided us in making recordings, took over the Scottish Festival Chorus and ultimately moved to France and trained choirs for Daniel Barenboim.

Singing for Arthur was an experience I had never known before and was – with one possible exception – never to experience again. We sang our hearts out and became a creative community, helping and understanding one another, ending rehearsals in eccentric public houses, travelling occasionally to cities other than Edinburgh and eventually taking a leading part in a European Festival of Sacred Music held in Cologne, where we gave the final concert with rare sixteenth-century Scottish motets arranged by Arthur. Occasionally I stood in for him as a conductor; now in Cologne I conducted the choir during a rehearsal so that he could hear how we sounded. I think that was one of the most unexpected and powerful moments of leadership I had ever experienced. Cologne itself was a lesson; I seized the change to visit the brilliantly restored and modernised churches that had been shattered during the war.

Even more absorbing, and for me educational, was a succession of journeys and commissions at home and abroad. Michael Gough, lecturer in classical archaeology in the University, recruited me one summer to join his excavation of a Roman basilica at Knossos on the Isle of Crete. I stayed in the British School of Archaeology in Athens and both then and subsequently seized the chance to visit classical ruins there and throughout Greece, especially at Mycenae and Delphi. I attended several summer schools promoted by Constantinos Doxiadis, the founder of *ekistics* (the science of human settlement) and joined one summer a cruise (financed by him) through the Mediterranean, stopping at several islands and culminating at Delos for the approval of what came to be known as the Delos Symposium.

The key figure in much of this and many other activities was of course Robert Matthew. He was a keen follower of ekistics, was a personal friend of Doxiadis and became the president of the International Union of Architects. He was also, in the 1950s, president of the Royal Institute of British Architects. Because of his international reputation and that of his office, he was invited to be the official British competitor in an international competition, 'Haupstadt Berlin' in 1957 – a great public gesture aimed at the reunification of the divided city.

This was before the building of the notorious Berlin Wall, separating East and West Berlin. But administratively the Russian sector was quite different from the unified British and American sectors. Matthew set up a design team of selected members of his office, several private architects and me as project coordinator. We met in the Department of Architecture and produced all the necessary plans. To study the city, two of us flew to Berlin and stayed there for two weeks, exploring both West and East and consulting the planning authorities. I read as much as possible and wrote the report. We did not win. But I seized the chance to study in some detail the comprehensive area of new housing designed by architects from many parts of the world in the Tiergarten area of the city. And I was responsible for devising a traffic system in a multi-level city centre as part of our competition design.

Back in Edinburgh I devoted myself to the education of

myself as much as a brilliant group of students who attended my tutorials and discussed not only art and architecture and town planning but many other subjects which seemed to me essential to any reputable education. I convinced myself that I now belonged to Edinburgh – and loved it.

It was, ironically, the problems of the Housing Research Unit which led me to leave. Once again, as in the School of Scottish Studies, the unit was riddled with dissension. Ultimately it had to be completely reorganised. For the time being, Matthew tried to solve its problems by getting rid of an active member of the team. I thought him wrong and in the course of a protracted argument, offered my resignation. Matthew rightly accepted it and I walked off down the Square, feeling a sense of freedom and justification. The first person I met was a senior lecturer in art history who asked me why I was looking so happy and when I told him, said that he had an idea for me. A new university was about to be founded in York and they might need someone like me. It was another turning point. Although Robert Matthew subsequently rejected my resignation and asked me to stay, the wheels of change were already beginning to turn.

It was just as well. I loved Edinburgh and still do; but recognised that I and the family must move to a new place, however often we would constantly return.

The quarrels in the Housing Research Unit had destroyed my belief in the dispassionate love of learning and one of my students had killed himself; another had a disastrous nervous breakdown, Biddy's eldest sister had been certified and I had taken her to hospital. I was ill. In a moment of acute depression and incipient breakdown that left me with 'tunnel vision' and the temptation to kill myself, I drove into the Lammermuir Hills one day and sat by a stream near the Cistercian abbey of Nunraw, and wrote this poem:

> Lord that I may see
> Darkness has come upon my sight
> And in my mind
> Let not this night

81

This dark dark night
That makes me intolerably blind
Let it not hold me endlessly
Lord have mercy on me.

Lord that I may see
As once a blind man called to thee
Hold me for safety in your hand
Let me but understand
Lord have mercy on me.

As once a blind man cried to Thee
Lord, Lord that I may see.

3

The Formation of a University

We moved to York in January 1962. By that time we had four children. For a week or two they and their mother stayed in the house at Glasyers while I rearranged a house in York that we were to borrow for a few months. Then they joined me and we began a new phase in our life, a phase which was the most exciting and totally absorbing experience I have ever had. It was nothing less than taking a critical part in the formation of a new university.

Whatever it may have been for the other participants, for me it was in every way a new life. I had been grossly overworked in the department in Edinburgh, devising courses and running a department in the frequent absence of its Professor, as well as trying to make money by writing articles for a newspaper. On top of that I had been profoundly upset by the vicious quarrels in the Research Unit. All of this, the illness of one of the children and the well-known trauma of moving a family to a new house (as well as buying it) reduced me to a state of nervous exhaustion. Perhaps what I needed was a new scene. Here, in another stunning but very different ancient city, was opening up a whole new prospect.

To explain that new prospect, a few words are necessary. When, shortly after the end of the war, a small group of public-spirited people in York formed a Civic Trust and approached the government to suggest that York should have a university, the reply was that there was no need for one; but that if that policy were to change, preference would be given to any town or city that showed initiative and proved that it could foster academic activities. York Civic

Trust, which is older than the national Civic Trust and is still a major force in the city of York, had been set up both to preserve and improve the city and help its development. One of its first actions was to establish an academic committee which soon became the York Academic Trust. It founded two institutions: the Borthwick Institute of Historical Research, which housed the archives of the archdiocese and other bodies, and the Architectural Institute, which initially arranged studies and courses on the care of churches and the protection and repair of historic buildings. The Trust took over two ancient buildings in the city centre which would otherwise be redundant.

St Anthony's Hall, a former mediaeval guildhall, became the Borthwick Institute for Historical Research, and the empty St John's Church, Ousebridge, became at first the York Institute of Architectural Study and later (and sounding grander) the Institute of Advanced Architectural Studies. Its Secretary, who was also secretary of the Borthwick Institute and the Academic Trust, was John West-Taylor, a graduate of Cambridge who had done national service in the navy. He started the activities of the architectural institute with a series of summer schools and short professional courses. They were conducted at first by members of staff from the Department of Architecture in the University of Manchester. One of them, Dr Singleton, was in due course appointed the first full-time Director of the Institute and moved to York only to die six months later of leukaemia. They had to find a new Director.

By that time, as a result of a major study of potential student demand (the Robbins Report), government policies had been reversed. At the end of the 1950s, and the beginning of the 1960s, a number of new universities were founded. The first was at Brighton, the second at York and, at the same time, new universities were founded at Warwick, Essex, Norwich and Lancaster, delightful and historic towns rather than great industrial centres.

The first action of the new University of York was to incorporate the Borthwick Institute and the Institute of

Advanced Architectural Studies. It was therefore necessary not only to find a Director for the Architectural Institute but also to bring it within the new university. I had met John West-Taylor while attending a summer school at the Institute. He now decided that I would be a suitable Director. I was interviewed by the Vice-Chancellor designate, Lord James of Rusholme, in his study at Manchester Grammar School and came to York to direct the Institute, take it into the University and play a part in the foundation of the new university. It was all agreed informally. As far as I can remember, I never had a letter of appointment.

From the very start I had to ask myself some basic questions. Why did we need new universities? As a result of the studies carried out for the Robbins Report on higher education, it had become clear that the numbers in higher education ought to be much higher than they had been before. The fundamental principle announced in the Robbins Report was that there should be 'a place in higher education for every boy and girl who was qualified to take it, and wished to do so'. To satisfy what must be a massive demand, they could either enormously increase the size of the existing universities or found new ones. Edinburgh University, for example, decided to double its size.

But there was a serious problem. Not only in Edinburgh, which as I recorded in the last chapter, destroyed a valuable Georgian square, but in almost every other major university city, there were intractable difficulties in finding new sites close to the existing university for new departments and new residences. In the hope of avoiding some of the fierce battles in university cities, government policy, expressed through the University Grants Committee, was that a new university would only be established at the request of a local authority which could offer a site of some 200 acres unobstructed by existing buildings. All the new universities were, as a result, outside their cities. The site for the University of York was the nearest to the centre. It would occupy 185 acres in a wedge of clear land just within the built-up area in the south-east.

For me it was a necessary change. I had been deeply depressed by my experience of academic warfare in Edinburgh. Suddenly, here was a new opening. I became Director of the Institute, Reader in the University and a member of the initial group of academics, all of whom had been head-hunted rather than applying for the job.

None of us was at that stage celebrated academically, but we were a very interesting and adventurous group. We included Harry Rée who had been a war hero, working with the Resistance in France, and then Headmaster of Watford Grammar School; Philip Brockbank, who became Professor of English; Graham Moodie, who became Professor of Politics; and (a little later) Wilfred Mellors, composer and musicologist who became Professor of Music. The only recruit who had already been a Professor was Alan Peacock, who had been Professor of Political Economy in Edinburgh and now became Professor of Economics at York. What did we have in common? Only, apart from our relative youth, the fact that while we had all carried out research and recognised its importance, we were essentially involved in *teaching*.

When I arrived in York, the University consisted only of the Vice-Chancellor, Lord James, the Registrar, John West-Taylor, a few administrative staff and myself. The other academics who had been appointed were not due to take up their appointments for another six months. What intervened was a series of what James called 'long weekends' when we would gather on a Friday, stay till the Sunday evening and have long discussions, organised and led by James, on the nature of the University, what it might do, what would be some of its problems, how it should be structured and how we might work out the implications of the principles outlined by the advisory committee which had reported on the setting-up of the University.

It was a rare and exciting experience. I commuted for a year between Edinburgh and York, first living in Edinburgh and commuting to York, then living in York and commuting to Edinburgh. I took over the Institute, founded new courses and played an active part in the discussions about the new university.

It soon became obvious to me that there were at least two conflicting concepts of a university among us. The Vice-Chancellor was a brilliant teacher with an idea. It was, I suppose, a Platonic idea. He was a devotee of Plato, whose aphorisms were used on many occasions either to back up arguments or to raise questions as we pursued our discussions. We, or perhaps James alone, would constantly refer to Newman's *Idea of a University* – at that time one of the few fundamental texts we could use to discuss the nature of learning and the nature of higher education. As far as I remember we did not refer to Whitehead's *Aims of Education and Other Essays* which later became essential to my own educational philosophy.

The Vice-Chancellor's concept of the university was based upon his experience as a student at Oxford, and then of teaching, with great brilliance, in very good schools – first Winchester and then Manchester Grammar School, of which he became the High Master. He had become a member of the powerful University Grants Committee. He saw the University as a social/academic unity pursuing excellence, sufficient unto itself, independent and autonomous. Its social life would be an essential balance to its academic studies; so we would have colleges, to one of which every member of staff as well as every student would belong.

On the other hand, Alan Peacock, the only academic recruited at the start who was already a Professor, who was later to become well-known for the Peacock Report on the BBC's finances, was a single-minded specialist. Where James was concerned with the unity of the whole, Peacock was concerned with the excellence of its component parts, in his case the Department of Economics. Enough excellent departments would add up to an excellent university.

I have forgotten much of the discussions that took place. What sticks in my mind are the pragmatic things: for example, the discussion about the nature of departments. In my next role the decision would be different; at this stage there was no question of the type of departments we would set up: they would be departments based not upon activities or vocations but upon subjects, or disciplines. We would have departments of English, History, Mathematics, Philosophy, Economics, Politics, Sociology, Physics, Chemistry and Biology. As soon as possible there would be a Department of Music. That introduced a different kind of activity, which had something in common with architecture, described once as 'frozen music'.

One of the inherent weaknesses in the plan was, I thought, revealed by the problem of servicing between departments. James believed that service teaching by academics from one discipline of students taking another was almost always unsuccessful. The problem is fundamental and inescapable, given the usual academic structure of a university. If it is organised by disciplines and if the disciplines receive the money, the disciplines will be in control and genuine collaboration between them will be minimal. But nearly all serious social development nowadays involves more than one subject and is interdisciplinary.

Just as influential were the work and attitude of the architects for the site and the new buildings. Whatever happens in the case of existing institutions, it must be the case that in the formation of a university, especially a new university on a greenfield site, the decisions of the development planners – the architects – must limit the possibilities of, or even prevent, what can happen. Although the academics often denied this, I felt sure that the architects for the development had a profound effect upon the academic development.

The architect for the University of York had been Chief Architect in the Ministry of Education, where in the post-war years they had developed not only systems of prefabrication, but an approach to the design of buildings based upon as precise as possible a performance specification. In this they were unlike most of the academics, even though we were more buccaneers than typical academics. In the academic mind there is a great advantage in indecision; it enables one to retain a reputation for calmness, judgement and independence. It is at the moment when one has actually to do something and make a decision about a place or a thing that one's reputation for impartiality is destroyed.

Some important decisions about the University of York were, I believe, made by the architects, however much in consultation. For example, it was early decided that departments would be in separate little buildings reached from walkways between colleges, never big enough to house all the staff in that particular subject; the rest would be dispersed among the colleges. After much discussion it was decided to put the departments into the colleges, but they would never be complete. Some members of staff would be in a different college from the Professor. The exception to this was economics; to meet the Professor's demands a special building had to be put up for economics as well as the adaptation of an older building for its research unit.

Looking back on it now, there seems to me an interesting contrast in success and failure. James's basic plan was, I believe, an overall success. The colleges were, in his phrase, a tender plant, but they had a reality and an identity from the start, which created an atmosphere and a sense of community that made York remarkably free of student trouble of any serious kind at the end of the 1960s. On the other hand, the isolates in Economics were one of the few groups that had a serious sit-in during those tempestuous years. The initial grouping together of the Social Sciences (Economics, Politics and Sociology) as a unity was illusory. And that was for me an important recognition which had a bearing on my subsequent academic plans. In a complex university the components are not really the simple ones that feature in a plan. We might group ourselves into faculties, which is broadly what the economists tried to do by grouping together economics, politics and sociology. But faculties are frequently artificial; the realities, if one is going to teach by subject, are the subjects or disciplines.

It was mainly, I think, on advice from John West-Taylor,

that the University recruited as its architect and planner Stirrat Johnson-Marshall, a recognised expert on the planning of school buildings and grounds. He in turn recruited Andrew Derbyshire as the project architect for the University. I watched the plans being drawn up and took part in many discussions.

Our new university was to be a collegiate university. Its planner might not be a great designer but he was a superb analyst. He demanded, from Eric James and from all of us, answers to all sorts of fundamental questions. What emerged was a design for a university of limited size with a strong socio-academic character. The brief from the University Grants Committee was that the University should grow to a size of 3,000 students. It was early decided that approximately 2,400 of these would be undergraduates and 600 would be graduates.

If there were eight colleges, each college would have 300 students, half of whom would live in college and half would have to find lodgings in the city – a considerable advantage to the city. It was thought – and we were given advice by a senior catering officer in the Ministry of Education – that 150 residents would economically support a kitchen and dining room which could also cater for 150 outsiders. It was decided that every member of the University (staff as well as students) should be a member of a college. Each college would have a dining-room big enough for 300, common rooms, study bedrooms, a library and, of course, a bar.

It was at this point, or possibly a little earlier, that Stirrat Johnson-Marshall had the most brilliant architectural idea of the whole project. He knew that the land given to the University at Heslington, behind and around Heslington Hall, was seriously waterlogged and would have to be drained before any building could commence. His brilliant idea was not just to drain the water away into the nearest river, but to dig out an enormous shallow bowl which would become a lake. The lake created at Heslington occupies about fourteen acres. Unlike traditional lakes, bottomed by puddled clay, this lake was kept in existence with sheets of polythene welded together by a blowlamp. It was filled partly from a local stream but mostly from the drainage of the site. I still remember being told about the idea before anything was done and being astonished and delighted by it. It was, in fact, the single biggest architectural idea behind the whole development. The colleges were grouped irregularly around the lake.

The landscape architect who advised not only on the lake but on the whole landscape was Frank Clark, who had been recruited to Edinburgh by Robert Matthew. He and I had met in slightly bizarre circumstances at the end of a rather drunken party in Matthew's office when I climbed up and sat on the crossbar of a street lamp and had a philosophical conversation with Frank standing on the pavement below. He stayed with us whenever he came to York, brought presents for the children and never failed to leave some of his belongings behind when he left.

The final physical element which linked all the components together was a decision also taken at the very beginning. That was to build covered ways between all the buildings, pedestrian routes which would go not only between buildings but through the heart of each college. A rough calculation showed that by any of those routes it was possible to get from one building to any other building in ten minutes. If lectures started at five minutes past the hour and finished at five minutes before the next hour, it would be possible to take many different combinations of subjects. There would be no faculties but a constantly changing pattern of disciplines.

The development plan for York University was recognised from the start as an authoritative publication. It was essentially a rational plan for growth, not a plan for a fixed environment. In a sense, its only fixed element was the lake; all the other elements could change and grow and be modified. It was decided that, with the exception of certain spcialised buildings like a central hall for assemblies and examinations and the laboratories for chemistry, physics and biology, all the colleges would be built using a prefabricated system originally developed for schools in conditions of mining subsidence. Such schools were contructed with a light steel frame, flat roofs and cladding panels of man-made materials. This system was CLASP, acronym for Consortium of Local Authority Special Programmes. Disloyal architects said it meant 'collection of loosely assembled steel parts'. The system required that no building would be higher than four storeys; no building would have lifts; no building would have unique or distinctive features. It was an environment of ordinary, anonymous, repetitive social buildings. They were not the cheapest but they had one great advantage which was exactly what the University needed; the buildings were on time and on cost. Eric James said, 'I am not prepared to stand on the platform at York station and say to the students just arrived, "I am terribly sorry but your buildings are not ready".' Almost uniquely for a university, they were on time. In summer the campus became a kind of Arcadia. The Institute of Advanced Architectural Studies housed its summer schools there, and the University soon became one of the most popular sites in the country for conferences.

Looking back on those early days of the University, I recognise the extraordinary privilege of being part of that society and a participant in the development of a wonderful environment. The landscape became richer and more varied with every year. All the trees that could be saved on what became a building site were saved. Hundreds more were planted and shrubberies and bushes began to soften the austere new buildings.

The architects donated the first ducks which instantly flew away; for the next pair a ceremony beside the lake welcomed them as our first tenants. Swans seemed to find their own way there, fish multiplied, insects hurried along to share the scene, birds flew over and landed on the buildings and on the lake. I wrote for the student magazine an article called *The Pond*, the intellectual centre of *Animal Farm*. Students clambered around the colleges and fell into the lake. We were economical with the buildings, more generous with the landscape, hospitable to every idea, tolerant of every absurdity.

It seems almost inexplicable now. The senior common rooms in the colleges each had a cupboard full of drinks. We could help ourselves, fill in a bill and have the money deducted from our salaries the next month. Conversations in the early evening before dinner were some of the best I have ever known. Rich in ideas, very funny and sharply witty, they created a kind of university atmosphere that probably never existed in any other university except in novels.

Even academic meetings were enjoyable. James suggested that every regulation should contain the word 'normally' so that we could always ignore or change it. He suggested that meetings should only be held if the issue could not be resolved by an individual.

Apart from our own work, we were constantly involved in interviewing candidates for all sorts of academic and related jobs. They were conducted in the most informal way, often sitting in armchairs after a friendly lunch. Eric James once remarked that on one occasion, apart from himself and the candidate, all the interviewing panel were asleep.

If that gives an impression of irresponsible slackness, I must correct it by insisting that in all this cheerful informality the University was governed and administered in a most efficient manner. James was a witty but masterly Chairman of the Academic Board and the Professorial Board. John West-Taylor, who had moved on from the Academic Trust to become Registrar of the University, was almost ruthlessly efficient. He spoke little, having a slight speech impediment, and his office work was rapid and thorough. He seemed to complete it early in the day, leaving him free to take part in University decisions of all kinds. He was concerned about details and demanded the highest standards of interior decoration, with natural colours and materials. He and James formed a rare team in university management.

And I found many ways in which I could contribute my

Conference sketches, York

own skills to the fledging university. I helped colleagues to read and understand plans (people often pretend to understand them when in fact the reading of plans is an acquired skill); I drew out notices such as 'No Smoking'; more significantly, at the request of John West-Taylor, I designed the first University Prospectus, choosing the typefaces, specifying the layouts and correcting the proofs. I also agreed with him designs for stationery and reports.

The University also introduced me to Yorkshire as well as York. I gave lectures in Middlesborough and many other cities, towns and villages. Of all those experiences one of the most absorbing was the term I spent in Ribblesdale. The Professor of Education, Harry Rée, had been recruited as Provost for one of the colleges and sold his house in

94

York and bought a disused farmhouse at Colt Park, close to the famous railway viaduct that crosses the moor near Ribblehead. With a richly deserved sabbatical term, I explored the dale with Biddy, wrote my first TV programme and took most of the family on the romantic Settle-Carlisle railway. In those days I smoked heavily, mostly small cheroots. Having accidentally left them behind and failed to borrow any from a friend I spied on the platform, I decided while sitting on that wonderful train that this was a message that I should give up smoking and on our return burnt my cigarettes and never smoked again.

Meantime, while taking part in the planning and growth of the University, I was busy directing and elaborating the work of the Institute of Advanced Architectural Studies. Whereas it had at first run short courses on the protection and repair of historic buildings as well as summer schools about, for example, the English Country House and Garden, I introduced a much wider range of new courses for architects and others, on Developments in Quantity Surveying, Cost Control, Library Planning, Hospital Planning, the Economics of Central Area Development, Arbitration, Landscape Reclamation and many aspects of Architectural Management. The Institute itself, in the mediaeval church of St John Ousebridge, bubbled with activity. And it acquired a national – and then an international – reputation.

St John's Church had been brilliantly restored, at first by George Pace, the most scholarly and original architect in York, expert in both restoring old buildings and designing new ones, and then transformed into a centre for lectures and discussions and social contacts by Dr Singleton, its first Director. It had a superb lecture room which could easily be rearranged, and in my opinion the best architectural library outside London. All the fitments were beautifully detailed and meticulously maintained. We were a small staff. At first myself and a lecturer/departmental administrator, who left after a few months and thus enabled me to reorganise the place and appoint my own staff. I now had an administrative assistant as Secretary of the Institute, a

Research Fellow and three young secretaries as well as a porter/cleaner. Later I persuaded the University to appoint an Assistant Director, who took over as Director when I left.

We were a happy team, working hard, laughing and talking, sometimes taking out a boat and rowing up or down the Ouse, leaving a note on the door saying 'Back in five minutes'.

Apart from its hospitality to local societies and entertainments, the work of the Institute became more and more varied. The short courses had a lot in common, whether already established or devised by me. All the courses were professional, technical and specific. They were short courses attended by architects and planners, builders and engineers, and many other professionals associated with the creation and management of the environment. Of the courses invented by me some of the most interesting were about economics in central area planning; some of the most exciting were exercises in professional collaboration – designing a building with all the different professionals involved following a systematic plan. Some of the most radical were courses and seminars on teaching methods.

That was an idea of mine that had, I suppose, been planted in my mind when I attended classes in both the University and the College of Art in Edinburgh and grew more urgent as I sat in on so many interviews for the new university. Some university lecturers were brilliant, the majority no more than adequate, some really disgraceful. The strange thing was that university teachers were not expected to be trained as teachers; their scholarship was the reason for their appointment. They tended to read their own lectures and sometimes hand out notes. I had read critical comments by Jane Abercrombie who was attached in a research capacity to the Royal Institute of British Architects, and recruited both her and Dr John Morris, psychologist in the Manchester University Business School, to devise practical exercises in teaching methods for architectural and other teachers. Architects who attended them would often tell me later that the courses (abandoning from the start the conventional lecture format) had changed them into professional teachers, no longer just practising architects putting in the occasional appearance in a school of architecture.

When I left the Institute at the end of the 1960s I summarised the educational work that I had arranged and supervised. Apart from more than thirty summer schools on aspects of architectural history we had run more than 100 professional courses for architects, planners and builders. In round figures we had organised 150 courses attended by 5,000 participants and 800 lectures. Summer schools had lasted a week or a fortnight, professional courses (at first long weekends then midweek) lasted four days, usually one every fortnight. I calculated that about 20 per cent of the architectural profession in Great Britain had attended the Institute in my time there.

From early in that period it became increasingly clear to me that mid-career people coming on a professional course could not be fobbed off with generalities of a conventional academic kind. The lecturers and organisers of seminars and discussions had in the main to be people from practice; the subject-matter had to be immediate and practical. The fact is that both in the planning of professional courses, in the subject-matter, and in the way in which they are run, mature people need to rediscover reality. And that, for most people trying to earn a living, means a reality that has to do directly with their existing mode of life and with the extension of its possibilities. The call for quality had to be a part of the development of efficiency, competence and satisfaction in the ordinary round of daily work.

It followed from this that the Architectural Institute occupied a somewhat eccentric place in the University of York. I could not avoid the conclusion that had the University of York been founded first it would not have found it necessary to develop an Institute of Advanced Architectural Studies. On the other hand, architecture was central to the city of York. We could run courses on the restoration of old buildings, on the management of projects and on the problems of organising the reassembly and redevelopment of old environments; but the city of York was itself an architectural masterpiece that offered very real problems that ought to be solved. There was, for example, the real problem of town planning in York and the conservation of its buildings, which became a crisis in the mid-1960s and in which I played a part in provoking the arguments and discussion which led ultimately to a changed policy.

While the University as a whole kept at first its distance from the city and occupied itself on the site at Heslington, described by the Vice-Chancellor as an offshore island, the members of the Institute of Advanced Architectural Studies engaged in activities and controversies provoked by the change of the actual environment in which we were living and working. As we did so, it became clear to me that it was valuable for any academic community to be involved with the community as a whole, and for the community as a whole to be involved with it.

I became angry at the way in which, it seemed to me, the city of York was being ruined by new, faceless office blocks. I provoked a public controversy by resigning from the city's Architects Advisory Committee of which I had been made a member and writing an open letter to the local paper which received national publicity. It coincided with a national change of view, much influenced by the National Civic Trust (younger than York Civic Trust).

By the end of the 1960s, what I saw as an attempt by York to turn itself into a modern city was reversed; it now became famous not for *development* but for *conservation* – that is, both preserving and enhancing an environment. The Civic Amenities Act was passed in 1967 and established the need for conservation *areas*. In that process, a major event was the publication of a plan for conservation commissioned by the Government from Lord Esher. In the University we organised a major conference on Towns and Cities, devised and presented by three students in consultation with me.

Although relatively a foreigner, I had already begun to

feel a citizen of York. Although apparently fit and full of energy, I was still partially crippled, with a back support on my back and a short caliper on one leg. I reported to the hospital and had my back support replaced by a surgical belt, which I still wear. I walked everywhere, especially round the walls.

I had in fact been in York before. During a summer vacation I had accompanied my father to a church in Lancashire to fix a stained-glass window and we then drove across the Pennines and spent a day in York, mainly looking at stained-glass windows. York has the biggest number of such windows in Britain and its Minster is veritably a huge lantern of stained glass, mostly of the fourteenth and fifteenth centuries. I decided that the great East Window, the size of a tennis court, was possibly the greatest work of art in the world and the windows in All Saints North Street the most original and evocative. We visited a stained-glass artist in his studio and met the Dean.

So, when shortly after my move to York both the Dean and his architect, Sir Albert Richardson, died at about the same time and the new Dean asked me to convene a small group and find a new architect/surveyor, I seized the opportunity of getting to know the Minster and its glass more thoroughly than I could before. I learned a lot about the personalities involved and about the architectural problems. We concluded our investigations by recommending Bernard Feilden of Norwich who was working on that cathedral and had restored and adapted the old buildings acquired by the University.

In my years at York and the Institute, only one thing failed. I had intended, in coming to York, not only to run a postgraduate institute and take part in the development of the University, but to found in that incomparable city an undergraduate school of architecture. Without a doubt, it would have succeeded; there could not be a better centre for architectural studies than the historic city of York. After a few years running courses at the Institute, I knew all the people I intended to appoint to the staff. And the essential arrangements had already been made. The library was superb, research projects were under way and I had set up an architectural office in the King's Manor (the design unit) to provide the practical training for students otherwise engaged in theoretical and studio work. The architectural reputation of York was well-known, we had applications from potential students who assumed that an undergraduate school was already established.

To accommodate the school we moved the Institute from its old church to the King's Manor, a superb ancient building in the centre of the city, beside the art gallery and only a short way from the Minster. With elements from many periods, it had been the abbot's house for St Mary's Abbey, become the offices and residence for the Council in the North set up after the Reformation and then a school for the blind in the nineteenth century. In order to provide study rooms for staff and students in the first years of the University, Bernard Feilden had completed a second quadrangle and made it apparently a traditional university building.

In 1967 the University Grants Committee decided that the country did not need any more schools of architecture and that therefore it would provide no money for one in York. It was a grievous disappointment to me and to the University. I could continue to direct the Institute and lecture in many other places. But short courses cannot ultimately provide a satisfying academic milieu. I decided to take my time, look around and possibly look abroad.

In the event I did not go far. At the same time as it rejected the proposal for an undergraduate school in York the University Grants Committee rejected a long-standing proposal in Leeds to transfer its School of Architecture from the College of Art to the University. In the confusion and uncertainty that followed I was invited by the Vice-Chancellor of the University and the Chief Education Officer for Leeds to chair a joint meeting of both bodies to decide what to do. By the time that committee had finished its work, it had been decided by both the Government and the local authority that four of its colleges should be amalgamated to form a polytechnic. I was asked to apply for the post of Director of Leeds Polytechnic.

Before I did so I thought hard about the meaning of a polytechnic and especially about why, after this involvement in the very meaning of a university, I should find this idea meaningful to me. I decided that it was more precisely what I had trained for. I theorised that, mainly through my father and his influence in steering me towards a college of art rather than a university, I was the product of two traditions.

Those two traditions in education had always been present in my life. On the one hand was education for its own sake, for the improvement and furnishing of the mind; on the other, education for a purpose, often acquired mainly through practical experience. That might be described as the difference between education and training (and the Royal Institute of British Architects [RIBA] had used the argument in justifying the move from colleges to universities). As a result of my experience in both the College and the University in Edinburgh I was the product of both. It became for me a duty – almost an obsession – to prove that they were not really opposites but could be part of a much greater personal formation. Now was the chance to prove the point and put my training to use.

But that is the next chapter in my story. What this chapter has so far ignored is my personal story and its links with another significant development. When we moved to York we picked up again on one of the main elements of my childhood. My life had been shaped and given emphasis by our proximity on top of the hill and our gradual involvement with Eric Gill and his extended family, of which I had almost become a member. After my mother's death during my first term at a boarding school I went often during the holidays to Pigotts and usually to the Tegetmeiers' household. I respected its head, Denis, and came to regard his wife Petra, Gill's second daughter, as a kind of stepmother. She was always there and always ready to make a cup of tea: 'Whenever a man calls in,' she said, 'make him a cup of tea.' Their children were of the same generation as us; we spent many holidays together, often at the Gill's converted monastery at Capel-y-ffin.

After my spell in hospital, I fell in love with Judith, the eldest daughter, while my brother Micky fell in love with the second daughter, Prudence. Judith married a delightful, lively and witty young man, Alfred Bradley, who was the producer of plays at the repertory theatre in High Wycombe. From there he moved to Leicestershire where he worked as a drama adviser for the local authority and then joined the BBC's north region as a drama producer for radio. He worked in Leeds, and he and Judith with their increasing family bought and restored a house in Bramham on the A1 about halfway between York and Leeds. I stayed with them briefly while looking for a home.

Alfred, with characteristic generosity, introduced me to actors and journalists and writers working with him for the BBC (he started a fascinating programme about creative writing called *The Northern Drift*) and found us a house in the nearest village, Clifford. It was an unusually Catholic village, with a Catholic primary school, a convent and a remarkable Catholic church, built in the 1840s in Norman style.

Our house, which had been empty for several years, was on the main street, large and square, with three main rooms, four bedrooms and an attic, which I made into a studio. It had a useful back yard and a small front garden. Its name, Providence House, had been given to it by nuns on their way to found the convent.

Our children attended the Catholic school, as did the Bradleys. We soon had another three children, born in York. A boy from an orphanage in the next village, Boston Spa, asked me if he could stay with us when he had to leave the home at the age of fifteen; so we fostered him and thus had a family of nine. At secondary-school age they attended schools in York and Leeds and Harrogate. It seemed as if we were in the midst of a kind of poly-centric region, about halfway between London and Edinburgh, and halfway

Margaret Mead, anthropologist. Ekistics Symposium, 1971

between York and Leeds. I travelled to many towns and villages, especially after Alfred Bradley introduced me to the BBC.

It was the controversy about York, its development and its future, which led to my becoming professionally involved for many years with the BBC. At the height of the controversy a camera team from the BBC's Manchester studio filming for the regional programme *Look North* in Leeds interviewed me and the Chairman of the City's Planning Committee. It coincided with a team from the BBC in Birmingham who were preparing a series on provincial England coming to York and asking me to talk about the city, its history and current problems. That interview led to many other contracts. I became a member of the BBC's Advisory Council for the North of England, was invited to write and make programmes on modern buildings for BBC Schools TV and to write and present a longer series for further education entitled *Living in Towns*.

From that moment I became for a time effectively the BBC's architectural expert. For *Look North* I made many short programmes about northern towns and cities; for

Schools TV I made a series entitled *The Art of Building* and then made individual programmes on arts subjects, including Landseer's *Monarch of the Glen*, Vermeer's *Guitar Player* and many others.

In addition, I began to take part in radio programmes. The chairman of a weekly programme entitled *A Word in Edgeways*, which was recorded on Friday afternoons in Manchester and broadcast on Saturday evenings, was a brilliant journalist, Brian Redhead. For a time I was the most regular participant and met many people – politicians, academics and broadcasters. Then I became half of the northern team for *Round Britain Quiz*, one of the most puzzling and fascinating of all intellectual games.

Redhead was one of the most inexhaustible talkers I have ever known. He had an endless fund of scurrilous stories about well-known people. These stories entertained us at lunch but were not introduced into the programme. In the early days, we agreed the subject-matter for discussion when we met at luncheon. Later a new producer fixed the subject-matter in advance. Redhead had a fertile mind and a passion for the environment. Only once did we disagree about anything significant. I found him intellectually challenging; he insisted that I was even more so.

After *A Word in Edgeways* was wound up, Redhead worked for Breakfast Radio and became one of the most familiar personalities in the country, devoted to the North of England. He died in 1994, having by then become Chancellor of Manchester University.

When, as I shall describe later, I moved to Leeds I became more involved with the BBC than ever. I chaired a new northern advisory council which combined membership as disparate as Jimmy Savile and the Countess of Harewood. I wrote my first national TV programme as the British contribution to a European series to celebrate the country's entry to the Common Market. That programme was called *Towards Jerusalem* and was, I believe, a fair if colourful explanation of the Industrial Revolution. I made programmes about Leeds and York, about modern architecture and about town planning.

All this gave me a new perspective on education – all such presentations require more preparation than a normal lecture or class. But an especial gain for me was the introduction to a world of immensely able and often imaginative professionals. Whatever the situation, whatever the problem, everything had to work. In making programmes and in attending Advisory Councils I met outstanding people: managers, planners and actors. Some were idle, some were pretentious, the majority were admirable, inheritors and contributors to a modern tradition that made the BBC the greatest broadcasting organisation in the world. As I write this it seems doubtful if that reputation will be sustained.

Now, after some packed years at the Institute, discovering more every year about the problems of running an organisation, collaborating with other professionals and managing a team – and without an undergraduate school – I began to look around for a new challenge. I had discovered a capacity for broadcasting as well as teaching and managing; I had taken a junior and then more senior part in the founding of a university; I had begun more writing and met many writers. I needed a new challenge and more responsibility. And I found it without even having to move house.

4

The Formation of an Educator

The end of the 1960s was the beginning of the end of one of the most extraordinary and distinctive decades in the cultural history of the United Kingdom. For me, 1970 was the official beginning of a new adventure.

The planning and development of the new University of York had been an absorbing experience. The decision by the University to accept the University Grants Committee's recommendation that York should not have an undergraduate school of architecture meant on the other hand that sooner or later I would look for another post. I was not as devastated by the news as some of my colleagues expected; I was young enough at thirty-nine to look for another challenge. I thought of moving abroad. But the family was now (by modern standards) large and most of them were at school. It would be easier to stay in this country. I was certainly not ready to retire or even relax.

As it happened, we did not even have to leave Yorkshire. At the end of that extraordinary period of change, I found myself drawn into another educational experiment. I shall follow the arguments as they dominated my decisions and I discovered a role for myself in higher education. I had been an academic. I now became an *educator*.

I start this chapter with what was for me a memorable event.

My arrival to take over and be responsible for Leeds Polytechnic was suitably unpretentious. In my ordinary and unstylish car I drove around the Polytechnic's bleak and featureless ten-storey building near the centre of Leeds and its Civic Hall, and unable to find a suitable main entrance ended by driving into the only available space, the boiler-house yard. The boilerman, dressed in the appropriate boiler suit, hurried out and told me that I could not park there. I explained that I was the new Director. 'Oh, are you?' he replied. 'Well, in that case you can come in and inspect the boilers, because they have never worked properly since they were installed.'

So my first experience of the central buildings of Leeds Polytechnic was a few hours inspecting the boilers and meeting some of my fellow workers. My new post (which I was to retain for fifteen years) carried little if any status. That did not worry me. I had not left a university intending to create a similar establishment. A polytechnic, I thought, would essentially be a working community. As its chief, I decided to dress in what seemed to me ordinary, comfortable working clothes – no jacket and tie but ordinary slacks, a white shirt and a black jersey. 'How could I know you were the Director,' said a student one day, 'if you go around dressed like that? On second thoughts,' he added, 'just you dress the way you want!'

This section of my book is deliberately personal even if that makes it difficult to intersperse personal events and comments with more general issues which mattered to me as I became increasingly involved in national as well as local issues. This section is not only my own story, a history, analysis and personal memento, of an adventure in the growth and development of education in Britain which looked for a time like transforming attitudes and re-creating some of the values and abilities that had once made Britain the workshop of the world. The country was after all not only a nation of shopkeepers; it also provided the invention, the creative determination, that Britain pioneered and spread to every corner of the world.

And for a time it seemed that we were on the very edge of success – that the twentieth-century polytechnics had won through and established themselves as leading institutions in the national landscape of education. Their failure was for many people their success – in 1992 they were

Peggy

Susie Aug. 73

Jamie

Sandy

109

renamed universities. It is possible that they, or some of them, will retain the special characteristics that made them polytechnics rather than universities. But I doubt it. As an article in the *Economist* summed it up precisely, 'The government, by a simple if not fraudulent device, created new universities by changing a name'.

For me the setting up, organisation and management of a polytechnic was a great adventure. Let me summarise. I had played a significant role in the establishment of a new university department in the University of Edinburgh; I had then come south to York and been the first academic to arrive in a new university and take part in its growth from three people to 3,000 in less than ten years. That was an incomparable experience. What I now undertook (after a few years of looking for a new challenge) was nothing less than founding, or putting together, a major institution. The essential decisions had already been taken by Government both central and local. What I now applied for, and was charged with achieving, was the amalgamation of four colleges in Leeds – the Colleges of Technology, Art, Commerce and the College of Education in Home Economics – to form one polytechnic. That meant studying and deciding the meaning of the term 'polytechnic'. I left York University and threw myself into this great adventure. And from the start I recognised that I was in uncharted and troubled waters.

By 1969, I had decided that I could not indefinitely run the Institute of Advanced Architectural Studies in York. Short courses are fascinating; they are short and quick and have to be well-structured; but they also become repetitive. I had devised new courses on such subjects as the economics of central area planning, landscape reclamation, academic library design, hospital design and many courses in management. But after several years, there was nothing a lecturer could say that I had not heard before. So I had to look for new work. I was still interested in undergraduate schools of architecture, but my own interests had widened considerably.

Village in Swaledale where many of the sketches of the children were drawn

It happened this way. At the same time as it was decided by the University Grants Committee that there should be no undergraduate school of architecture in York, it was also decided that the School of Architecture in Leeds, which was in the local authority's College of Art, should not be transferred to the University, as had been intended for some fifteen years. The decision was a disastrous blow for experienced members of the School of Architecture. The Head resigned. The University was uncertain about its obligation and it was therefore decided by the Vice-Chancellor of the University and the Chief Education Officer of Leeds that a joint committee should be set up to review the situation and make recommendations for the future. They invited me to chair that joint committee and at the same time I was appointed Hoffman Wood Professor of Architecture at the University of Leeds – a visiting professorship which requires some three or five public lectures during the year and some incidental teaching in the School of Architecture. I gave a series on 'The Design of the Modern University', spent time

111

in the School of Architecture and became familiar with the administration of both the University and the local education authority.

After many months, the committee recommended that postgraduate studies in architecture should be undertaken by the University of Leeds, but that undergraduates should continue to attend a school run by the local authority. But now there was a difference. Whilst this was being decided, the Government had decided to found thirty new polytechnics. Leeds was to have one of them.

Although it was strictly informal, John Taylor (the Chief Education Officer) and Sir Roger Stevens (the Vice-Chancellor of the University) persuaded me to apply for the new post of Director of Leeds Polytechnic. I was quite indifferent as to whether I wanted to do it – which I suppose made me more convincing at the interview than I might otherwise have been. Anyway, by the summer of 1969 I had been appointed Director Designate of the proposed Leeds Polytechnic.

I have described my arrival. More seriously, soon after being appointed Director Designate I sought advice on how to run – or at least steer – a large and complex academic institution. I had seen, and shared in, Eric James's chairmanship of academic boards and committees; what I now needed was advice on the organisation and management of a democratic (or pseudo-democratic) body. I consulted John West-Taylor's deputy (and ultimately his successor) as Registrar, Anne Riddell.

Anne Riddell had had wide experience both in Britain and abroad, and been a major influence on the development of the University of York. She joined in many hours of discussion and gave advice when I pressed for it. One piece of advice was so important to the way in which I conducted meetings that I must emphasise it.

The most important statement or decision in any process is the first one. No matter how many modifications are made, no matter how many committees discuss it, no matter how various are the changes or profound the new understandings, they ultimately reflect that initial decision. She had, I think, learned that principle from a study of political history. I decided that all policies in the Polytechnic must be initiated by me and steered or modified through meetings. So my account of the Polytechnic's development has to be personal and I have to accept responsibility for it, even as I had to accept unwelcome changes.

The Polytechnic came legally into being on 1 January 1970. Although I had a broad idea of what that meant, I had no experience of local government education. I carried out considerable investigations of my own, but it was only when I received advice from authoritative sources that I began to understand the real significance of this educational development.

Shortly before I left York, the Vice-Chancellor of the University, Lord James of Rusholme, had been commissioned by the Secretary of State for Education and Science to review and report on teacher training. The Secretary of State was Margaret Thatcher. I had already met her and learned about her clarity of mind and power of decision. The Deputy Head of the Department of Education and Science was Toby Weaver (now Sir Toby Weaver). He was in effect the inventor of the polytechnics and the senior government administrator who most influenced their formation. Eric James sent me to see him. When I was ushered into his room, he was arguing on the telephone with Mrs Thatcher's secretary and insisting on seeing her to correct something. He put down the telephone and said, 'Best Secretary of State we have had for years.' We discussed polytechnics in considerable detail, I came to know him well and have remained, ever since, a family friend.

What he explained to me from the start was the essentially pragmatic nature of the polytechnic decision; the ideology would follow later. He had drafted the speech made by Anthony Crosland at Woolwich in 1965 which announced the change in Government policy. The pragmatic justification was simple: since the numbers of boys and girls entering higher education would, it was thought, continue to rise, the Government was faced with several options. It could either found more new universities or it could look to the places where higher education was already being conducted. The local authorities were responsible for further education and training as well as for schools. In principle, therefore, the potential students were already attending institutions run by the local authorities.

It was simpler – and immeasurably cheaper – to transform the further education scene than to found new universities on virgin sites. But were was *further* education conducted? It was conducted in colleges of technology, commerce, art and teacher training. It became government policy, enshrined in the White Paper of 1966, to select some of the leading colleges and group them together to form thirty polytechnics. A typical polytechnic would, therefore, offer courses in technology, commerce, art and teacher training.

This had a further advantage. Whereas in the early 1960s it had been thought that any course of advanced study could only be of benefit to the country, it was becoming obvious that the country could not absorb many more graduates in the liberal arts and social studies. What was needed was training in practical subjects. To satisfy social demand it was necessary to elevate these studies to what came to be known as *higher* education rather than *further* education. This would require degrees. A new organisation responsible for approving courses for the award of degrees was designated: the Council for National Academic Awards (CNAA). A polytechnic would, therefore, submit to the Council its proposals for courses. The Council would investigate the proposals and the institution's facilities in great detail. If it approved them, the polytechnic would run and examine the degree courses and the CNAA would award the degrees.

I was captivated by that scene and studied it in even greater detail. There were, for example, certain implications that affected the scene fundamentally. The colleges of technology had started, in the first instance, as mechanical engineering institutions in the 1820s; colleges of art had been set up to train designers for industry in the 1840s; the

114

colleges of teacher training had been established to train teachers for state schools after Forster's Education Act of 1870; the colleges of commerce had mostly been set up in the 1890s to train boys and girls in shorthand, typing and bookkeeping. In short, all the colleges had a practical purpose and all their products were expected to go into industry or the professions. They were never intended to be prestigious and certainly not pompous. (It followed that nearly all the colleges were undervalued. For years afterwards, parents would be deeply distressed if their children failed to be accepted by a university and had to go to a college or a polytechnic).

And there was a further essential element in their character – they were local. It was clear to Toby Weaver and his colleagues in the Department of Education and Science that the new polytechnics, whilst offering degrees, must also continue to offer diplomas and certificates and remain local by recruiting, as widely as possible, part-time as well as full-time students. I decided in Leeds that whereas we might be parsimonious in accepting full-time students, we should accept all the part-time students with relevant qualifications. At the start of each academic year there was a scramble for such part-time places in courses that were mostly evening classes and sometimes part-time day classes.

Now let me look at how it all worked. An early decision I made was to ensure that all academic appointments would be made by my colleagues and me and not, as had previously been the case, by councillors on the local authority's Education Committee. My relationship with the local authority was usually friendly but always fragile. The situation was fundamentally unsatisfactory – a local body of amateurs responsible for a national demand. At first the leading local authority personalities, like Frank Marshall (later Lord Marshall), were critical but also creative and their senior officials often obstructive. And that could be dangerous. Since nearly all our money came from central Government via the local authority, it was relatively easy for the latter to keep some of the money instead of passing it on to the polytechnic.

As far as the local authority was concerned, I worked closely with the Chief Education Officer and the Chairman of the Education Committee. At my interview I insisted on having direct access to the Chief Education Officer. John Taylor, who had persuaded me to apply for the post of Director, was the most clubbable, shrewd, helpful and not very decisive man. He had worked for the local authority since the war. The Chairman of Education was Councillor Crotty (always known as Paddy), rapid-talking and exceedingly well-read.

That neat and friendly arrangement changed with local government reorganization in 1973–4. John Taylor retired and became for a time Chairman of the polytechnic's governors (who were composed of one third councillors, one third local worthies and one third academic staff – plus the President of the Students' Union and one or two of my senior colleagues). It was clumsy but workable. Its first Chairman, Granville Robinson, chosen with great care by John Taylor, was a decisive local manufacturer – Chairman and Managing Director of Yorkshire Imperial Metals (the Copperworks), who had a degree in classics from Oxford University. He was always, in an unpretentious way, shrewd and helpful. We never quite found a successor with his clarity of mind and critical awareness. Some councillors were sharp and decisive and we became friends as well as colleagues. Others were intellectually dishonest and destroyed any kind of mutual respect.

I was a member of council of the University of Leeds – where I attended meetings and took a minor part in its deliberations (we had enough problems of our own in the polytechnic). What I had not expected was that the University provided me with one of the most rewarding friendships I ever made. That was Edward Boyle, shortly to become Lord Boyle of Handsworth. What follows is based upon an article I wrote about him after his death.

When I read in the paper that Edward Boyle had been

116

appointed Vice-Chancellor of the University of Leeds and was due to take up the post soon after I was due to take up my post as Director of the Polytechnic, I wrote to him suggesting a meeting and was immediately invited to luncheon at his club in London. It was a memorable meal.

He assumed, as I later learned was typical of him, that I would know everything he talked about and that my knowledge would be every bit as great as his. Almost straightaway I made two errors. In answer to a tentative question I remarked that I was very fond of music and had been listening a few days before to Beethoven's *Fourth Symphony*. He wondered if I would agree that the repetition of the trio section in that symphony was one of those innovations by Beethoven that might not have had quite the effect, etc., etc. I remarked that great as was my knowledge of music it did not really stretch to that kind of discussion.

He discovered that I had taught in Scotland and enjoyed reading Scottish history. He had always suspected that had the Solemn League and Covenant been better drafted in one of its key sentences it might well have been possible to avoid some of the conflict, etc. I did my best to indicate how much I agreed with the general drift of the argument.

He was quite unconscious of the effect of his erudition. When he expressed concern that I was being silent (rather rare for me actually), I said I was just ruminating on the strange mutability of human affairs, and hurried on in case he had read the whole of Dickens (he had) with a brief reference to *The Idiot* (he had of course read the whole of Dostoievski so I gave that up as well). He knew all about architecture and had actually read Banister Fletcher.

At that luncheon he insisted that he was not giving up politics to go to the University with any sense of retirement or retreat. On the contrary: when he had been Minister of Education he had discovered that it was the great provincial universities like Leeds that were doing the bulk of the work in higher education; and that far from its being a retirement, he saw the job as a great challenge.

He entered upon it with enthusiasm and total devotion.

Without any attempt to dominate anyone he became part of the University, ambling around it, talking to students and academics with the same confidence in their educational standards that he had demonstrated to me, and sometimes reducing them to terrified silence. Once or twice academics asked me to sit beside him at lunch in case he knew all about their subjects.

He always insisted that he valued the cooperation between the University and the Polytechnic, and indeed towards the end of his life insisted that it had been one of the most satisfactory aspects of his time in Leeds. It was true in a negative sense. We were, from the start, agreed that it was not part of our jobs to duplicate work. I undertook not to start courses (other than those already in being) which were really the job of the University. To the occasional annoyance of the Polytechnic staff I stuck to my promises. I also warned him whenever I heard rumours that the University was thinking of starting something that was really our business. I then left it to him. I am still overawed by the skill with which on one occasion, and with no direction from him, the University discovered that it did not want to launch a course after all.

I took to seeking his advice when I did not know how to tackle something thorny. We had some discussions on radio about education. I reminded him during one broadcast that he had once made the point that if it were to be creative, higher education had to be rather messy in its organisation and he indicated with characteristic kindness that he thought that we had both been signally successful in achieving that aim.

It was about that time that he came to dinner in our house one evening and made an unforgettable impression upon the family. There were seven or eight children round the table, some of whom were doing O levels or A levels, and the conversation moved gently around. At some stage I must have got out a bottle of Malmsey and one of the children made a remark about drowning people in it like the Duke of Clarence and wondered idly when that had

Horsehouse, Coverdale

Bolton Castle, Wensleydale

China from New Territory

Pippa's house, Nova Scotia

ckie's house, Vancouver Island

e railway station, Kuala Lumpur

On the Ginan Canal

From the train on the Nullarbor Plain, Australia

happened. 'The seventeenth of February 1478,' said Boyle. It was a total conversation stopper. After that no one had the nerve to say anything. He did the washing up. He said he had washed up in other houses with children. I should have put him onto it earlier.

In a lecture which he gave in several places but which I heard in the University of York, Edward Boyle remarked that the one thing he felt guilty about, and was for him a failure, especially as a Vice-Chancellor, was that he had never written a book. I thought about that remark a lot at the time and was not altogether surprised when a few years later he withdrew from giving the Reith lectures. Writing a book (which is really what they entailed) was not his style. He was a wonderfully acute debater, conversationalist and manager of discussion but he did not, I believe, have an original or creative mind; his brilliance lay in coping with a tremendous range of information and opinion, sorting it out and making a unity of it. He had an extraordinary capacity for detail, and exceptional memory and power of analysis.

I shall always remember some of the conversations I had with him when he became ill and when it had become clear that there would be no cure. He several times assured me that he valued the fact that I always told him how he was looking, without reservation. One Sunday afternoon when he was looking particularly bad I asked him if he was afraid of death. He had found a resolution of his feeling in *The Dream of Gerontius* (which as it happens I do know fairly well), and we discussed in some detail that passage between Gerontius and the Angel when the Angel speaks – darkly – of the stigmata and the agony which thrilled through body and soul in that embrace. It was in the exquisite music at that point rather than in the words that he had found an understanding. He had, I believe, been through many a dark night and had found himself at peace.

'My word,' he said that afternoon as he characteristically helped me to a chair and took my stick, though he himself could hardly walk. 'If people were to see you and me walking together along a pavement in Leeds, they would be very worried about the future of higher education in this city.'

That episode occurred when he was dying and I had become increasingly crippled and eventually unable to walk without sticks. At the start of the Polytechnic, I was aware of nothing so much as optimism and had, I suppose, an almost embarrassing self-confidence.

I had found it necessary to declare my attitude to the new Polytechnic right at the start when, during my interview, I was asked if I had sufficient experience to tackle the administration of a large-scale institution. I pointed out that the Polytechnic was shortly to appoint a Chief Administrative Officer, and that I did not see my job as only an administrator; my role was to be the leader of the institution both academically and socially. The structure of the Polytechnic management that I eventually evolved, after several changes and developments, was that I should be supported by three Assistant Directors, each with a special responsibility for one area – academic, resources and personnel. It is possible that in this division of the work I was influenced by my own experience in the setting-up of York University; but in the organisation of the academic or teaching areas of the Polytechnic we broke new ground. That will become obvious later, as my story takes shape. For the moment I want to concentrate on some of the appointments we made that had a lasting effect upon the character of the place.

The Principals and Vice-Principals of the amalgamated colleges had been made Chairmen of Faculties. As soon as they left (or in one case was persuaded to go), we abolished Faculties and made different appointments. The administrative assistant who had worked on the amalgamation of the College, Anthony Hamblin, became Chief Administrative Officer (and later Assistant Director). Gordon Wright became Deputy Director responsible for resources and Brian Gent became Deputy Director responsible for academic affairs. They were not national figures but both local. Later we added Bill Stark (formerly in the Department of Management) as Assistant Director responsible for

120

personnel. We formed an efficient team, unpretentious but quick in decision-making and always friendly.

I spent much time and energy constantly modifying the layout of the office which we dominated (if that is the right word). I had never doubted that the secretarial staff of any active management are essential to its character and had to form part of the team. In Edinburgh I had worked closely with Dorothy Taylor, the Professor's secretary; at York, I had recruited a brilliant team – Prudy, Anita and Chris. Now in Leeds we appointed at first Judith Nicholson and then Anne Fairburn. In the friendly 'landscaped' office which I designed, they and two other women not only worked hard but created the most welcoming social centre.

Within a year of the Polytechnic's designation, we formed an important group for the hundreds of overseas students recruited for vocational courses. The Overseas Students Advisory Group (OSAG) was founded and steered by an Indian engineering lecturer, Sultan Sultan, with my wife Biddy as secretary. Impressed by the strong social ethos of the University of York, she had noted the almost total lack of such social links in the local colleges and started a succession of lunches for staff and their spouses. The plural of spouse we decided being 'spice', they were known as 'spice lunches'.

As in all organisations, meals were essential meeting places and we went to some trouble to make sure that they were well-run and produced good food. The main restaurant was open to all staff and students, there was a staff restaurant in the technology block and a suitably smart restaurant in the Home Economics and Institutional Management block (generally known as the Pud School). The two ladies who ran the school had their own private dining room and servant; I abolished that as soon as they retired, had the block linked to the main complex and made it open to all – to the delight of the predominantly female students. Later I occasionally invited colleagues from within and without the Polytechnic to breakfast. They were the best breakfasts ever prepared in Leeds.

Of the members of an increasingly active academic staff, several became close friends. One of these, Alan McGregor, was teaching on the courses of General (or Liberal) Studies which were a compulsory element in any course in Technology and Commerce, when I promoted him to Head of Department, amalgamated all such studies under the title 'Contemporary Studies' and created another landscaped department for tutorials and seminars. Alan had had a distinguished career in the Royal Navy and had a natural unselfconscious authority. He died young at the age of sixty and was mourned by all his colleagues – a cheerful and quietly critical gentleman whom all of us wanted to have on a committee or board. The staff of a general or liberal studies department are by definition a disparate group, many left-wing and at this time inclined to quote *The Thoughts of Chairman Mao*. Alan brought the most variegated people together.

This brings me to a few comments about the students. It was, I suppose, an eccentric time to undertake the management of a large educational institution at the end of the 1960s, for this had been the period when students in many parts of the world transformed themselves into aggressive, self-centred agitators. It was later described by an author as the 'rise of the student estate'. It reached its climax in Paris in 1968 when it seemed for a time that another French Revolution (this time based on an alliance between students and workers) was about to take place. In America, a student demonstration at Kent State University led the military to open fire and two students were killed. It may be that students generally were sufficiently shaken by that event that they ceased to agitate forcefully; my impression was that the great student movement began to fade away in this country when it first became known that graduates might never be employed.

The student movement of the 1960s was mostly in the universities. Unlike many of them, York University was relatively peaceful. 'We're ready to go,' complained a student leader to the Registrar, 'and you won't even give us the information on which to base our protest.' But it upset the Vice-Chancellor who had until then always been a much-admired and respected leader in education. The polytechnics did not experience student trouble until later – in the early 1970s. For no discernible reason the students in Leeds Polytechnic staged a 'sit-in' during the autumn of 1972, occupying the administration offices which I had reorganised as an open (or landscaped) office on the first floor of the main block. They brought in bedding and TV. I could not get to my own office for several weeks, went home and wrote a book. The sit-in came to an end when a few engineering students, who wanted to attend their classes, remarked that they would kill the student leaders.

It was an unprecedented and baffling time. Frightened by events, most authorities (Leeds among them) gave Student Unions unprecedented power and money. Two students became members of our Governors and the Union was free to spend its money with a freedom that the Polytechnic management never enjoyed. At one stage the Union used its money, supplemented by a loan from a local brewery, to buy a country hotel for student holidays!

The student leaders were usually unimpressive and wasted much of our time at meetings. Two were exceptional, and moved into good posts in local government after leaving. Others were pompous and nasty. It was important for the Polytechnic that relationships should be cordial. I made it a policy that my door would always be open to student representatives.

And indeed to any student or any member of staff. Even at my busiest, I never had to refuse an interview for more than a week. For most of the time I enjoyed excellent friendly relations with the students. For example, shortly after my arrival the Student President challenged me to announce my policy about drug-taking, which was increasing in most colleges and universities. I wrote and distributed a carefully researched paper on what I called 'the chemical aid to day-dreams', emphasising that drugs were illegal and that 'pushers' should be reported to me. The Union unani-

Queen Square, Leeds, was taken over by Leeds Polytechnic,
now Leeds Metropolitan University

mously condemned my statement; and the next day the
Student President came privately to thank me.

I had decided that, unlike a university, a polytechnic
should be informal and unpretentious as well as comprehensive. The first graduation was therefore in ordinary plain
clothes; very few graduands came. When I then changed my
mind and made academic dress compulsory for such cere-
monies (especially when they were held in the town hall)
everyone came. No matter what our political views, we all
want to wear fancy dress.

Those events and occasions are of course peripheral to
the central activity of any place of education – teaching and
learning. One of the great and colourful characteristics of a
polytechnic was the extraordinary – and I think unprecedented – diversity of courses and personalities.

Some of that diversity was inherited from the constituent
colleges – a diversity that I defined as 'polytechnic plurality'.
The constituent colleges had been organised in different

124

ways. 'Commerce' was based upon job-oriented courses; the staff had considerable involvement in private practice and in pursuing their own professional careers. 'Technology' was based mainly upon conventional disciplines organised as departments, but was riddled with an inferiority complex caused largely by the proximity of the University of Leeds with its big departments of civil, electrical and mechanical engineering. 'Art' had a great reputation, but despite it seemed strangely defensive. The teacher training college contained an efficient section in institutional management, but as far as teacher training was concerned had lower standards of entry than any other part of the Polytechnic. Constantly on the move despite my increasing disability, I visited all the departments possible.

But let me select and pursue briefly some of the problems we faced with art and design. If the best financed department was graphic design, which produced outstandingly good graduates, the most valuable, both socially and industrially, was three-dimensional design which was less well-financed but had admirable workshops which could make almost anything in wood, metal or plastic. The most celebrated was fine art. That department caused a public crisis.

It happened this way. My arrival at the Polytechnic coincided with one of the strangest periods known in art education and indeed in the meaning of art itself. Under a former Head of Department, Harry Thrubron, fine art in Leeds had acquired an international reputation, mostly for abstract design, and it now shifted or was shifted increasingly in the direction of what came to be known as 'performance art'. Its philosophy was fashionable and very persuasive. It taught that the essence of art was not the production of artefacts but personal self-expression. It followed that the challenge to both staff and students was to enable the art students not merely 'to do their thing' but make it forceful and meaningful. Traditional skills such as life drawing had virtually disappeared from the curriculum; for several years no models were employed. To most of the art students it was immensely stimulating; to other students and staff it was incomprehensible. To the public it could be notorious and scandalous.

The most celebrated and able lecturer specialising in 'performance art' was Jeff Nuttall, who had been appointed shortly before my arrival. He was the author of a powerful book, *Bomb Culture*, which brilliantly analysed the fundamental and lasting legacy of the dropping of the atomic bombs on Japan in 1945. He was a good teacher, provoking events and taking part in them himself.

Of a number of colourful incidents, let me select only one. A group of fine art students arranged a performance one evening entitled 'Violence in Society'. They occupied the fine art studio, filled it with a student audience and locked the doors. The first part of the performance consisted of a student with a sledgehammer smashing a television set to pieces (cheers). Along the side of the room were cages of white mice which, by this time, were charging around in a frenzy; suspended across the room were strings on which were perched budgerigars tied by one foot. One of the students then produced an air pistol and shot one of the budgerigars; the other budgerigars fell off their perches and were held by one foot, fluttering desperately. A girl in the audience felt so angry that she leapt to her feet, seized a log of wood and hit the student over the head. Blinded (he later said) by blood, he fired the rest of the pellets at the audience. Most were struggling to get out but found the door locked. Eventually someone smashed it down, the audience rushed out and the police were called. It was, said the leading student, a total success; it proved more about violence in society than anyone could possibly have expected.

That event was not alone. Among fascinating artefacts was a formerly black car painted completely yellow, a gas cooker that sprayed water rather than gas when turned on (North sea gas, I presume), lines drawn over the floor of a corridor and walls to indicate psychological tension, an enormous ten-foot-long plastic penis lying on the floor. ('I've never seen one like that,' said my nine-year-old son.

'Nor will you ever again,' I remarked.) At the end of one year, a girl ran naked down the stepped ramp from the art block and leapt over flares of paraffin-soaked rags. The external examiners sat below the ramp critically watching the performance. She received a first-class honours degree and had her photograph in the evening paper.

I have used these incidents from only one department to indicate something of the complexity of my job – and its fascination. I spent as much time as I could in the building housing art and design. You never knew what you might see.

Looking back now, I realise that the most fundamental decision that we made in the early years emerged from a protracted argument about the organisational structure of the Polytechnic. The essence of the problem was this. Should the components of a large institution be academic units of a traditional and conventional kind or should they be units characterised by the activity to which their work leads? In other words, was the institution as a whole composed of disciplines and subjects which could be combined for people aiming at a variety of careers, or was the institution as a whole to be formed from units which were themselves oriented towards practice, towards vocations? In practical terms, this meant that the academic units of the Polytechnic could be either subject-based departments (mathematics, physics, chemistry, biology, etc.) or course-based departments. This was a much more fundamental issue than it might appear at first sight, because the model adopted would give the key to the character of the institution to which the academic staff belonged. After long discussion we decided to base the Polytechnic structure upon courses. The departments became organisations for the initiation, running, management and examination of courses. This was in line with the reality of the situation. Courses were what the students joined. They did not come to a polytechnic to study a subject with a view to becoming academics if successful; they came to a polytechnic to engage in jobs in industry and the professions. It was therefore logical that they should follow a course which was specifically oriented to that end. For example, we launched the country's first degree course in Nursing.

With one or two exceptions, the main one being mathematics which spent most of its time servicing other departments, we therefore organised the Polytechnic as a group of course-based departments, modified later to become schools. There were eighteen schools, all of which had names which indicated their function, and all of which ran courses geared to professional work. It followed from this that in the main the staff of the schools would be drawn, not just from one discipline, but from a variety of disciplines.

I resisted the conventional structure of 'faculties' which would have tended to perpetuate the former colleges, and would have presented an unassailable barrier both to the development of a total polytechnic ethos and to innovative thinking about course-based work. (I add as an ironic note that faculties were introduced to Leeds Polytechnic in 1986 by my successor, Christopher Price, and, as I even more wryly note, they coincided almost exactly with the constituent colleges of fifteen years earlier. In sorting out what he frequently described as the chaos he had inherited, he thus destroyed many of my creative innovations.)

Another decision of profound importance concerned the size of the schools. In an institution the size of the Polytechnic (it was to grow in my time to about 10,000 students full- and part-time, and almost 1,000 academic staff) it seemed to me essential that the schools, as the working units to which students and staff belonged, should be of a humane size for both staff and students to identify with and work with. It was clear that I could not know the entire staff. It seemed to me essential that I should know all the Heads of schools and something of their family circumstances, and as many as possible of the Course Directors. Following Schumacher's then celebrated ideal that 'small is beautiful', I decided that the optimum size for a school was about 300 – a big enough socio-academic group for students to recognise and get to know each other without being isolated. With a staff/student ratio of 1:10 this number would result in a Board of Studies whose maximum size would be 30 – the largest number possible in my estimation for any meeting to be productive.

So the essential components of the Polytechnic were not colleges or residences but departments. The departments were the real organisations which the students joined; they might indeed spend almost all their study time in the department. It was therefore important to see the departments as social as well as academic units. As soon as possible, which effectively meant a few years, we ceased to use the former college names and had all the buildings labelled 'Leeds Polytechnic'. Some departments were moved. For example, architecture and town planning, which had been part of the College of Art, were now separated from art and soon became separate from each other. For some reason which I never understood, economics and languages occupied one department in the College of Commerce. We set up languages as a department of its own and called it international studies. We amalgamated economics and accountancy – possibly a mistake because they turned out to have little in common.

That dealt with the names of the teaching units. To make them real, something more fundamental was required. In a capitalist economy like ours, the reality is money. To have confidence, each unit must control its own money. Had the money for academic expenditure been allocated to the faculties (the former colleges), we would not have achieved much; we, therefore, removed the academic budget from the faculties (or colleges) and allocated it to the departments. The effect was dramatic.

At the announcement of the new budgets, it became clear to the departments how asburdly different their allocations were. One Head of Deaprtment later told me that he felt physically sick when he heard how much money had been going to the departments in the former College of Art. I

129

was myself astonished when I discovered how little had been going to the department of accountancy.

This comment requires an explanation, which may throw a little light on the oddity of local government provision. Any course which could be classified as advanced further education (AFE) qualified without question for a 100 per cent subsidy from central Government – money allocated by a committee entitled the Advanced Further Education Pool, into which all local authorities paid and out of which only those who ran AFE extracted. A course which was followed mostly by part-time local students might feature as further education but not advanced; it would, therefore, receive not a 100 per cent grant, but a smaller precentage. The challenge to a department was, therefore, to make sure (or argue) that all its subjects were AFE. Odd as it might seem to outsiders, everything in the College of Art was advanced. The local authority received a 100 per cent subsidy from the AFE Pool and the Art College was therefore able to spend lavishly.

At the time of my arrival, the department of accountancy received £10 per student per *year*; the department of graphic design in the College of Art had £6 per student per *week* for materials alone. I was so astonished by this that I checked with other colleges and polytechnics and found that their art departments were just as lavishly treated. It did not make them better; it merely made them more complacent. Not surprisingly, it was the College of Art which was the most unwilling to join the new Polytechnic. I decided that we could not celebrate the amalgamation of the colleges by cutting their grants so I kept the departments from the former College of Art on the same budget but increased the funds of other departments when inflation demanded. The new building for art was being furnished when I arrived. The expenditure on its furniture, including drawing boards, TV sets and radios and anything else thought relevant, was more than handsome.

Let me pursue the argument further. If you assume that a university is essentially a community of learning – the pursuit of subjects wherever they may lead irrespective of the consequences, and their pursuit to a greater and greater depth under, nowadays, the delectable title of research – in what way is a polytechnic different? I had no doubt that, not only because of the origin of the colleges but also because of contemporary needs, the polytechnics were essentially institutions for *teaching*.

I used therefore to distinguish between polytechnics and universities in this way. A university is a community of specialists engaged in learning; a polytechnic is a professional institution developing teaching skills and insights in the service of society. It follows that if the greatest success in a university is to obtain a first-class degree and be invited to stay in the university and become an academic, the greatest success in a polytechnic is to leave the institution and become involved in the organisation and management of daily affairs.

As one of my first innovations, I established a small unit entitled 'The Education Technology Unit', later renamed the Education Development Unit, not only to provide information and training in the use of the media, but fundamentally to arrange courses and services so as to improve the standards of teaching. I intended, as a personal ambition, to make Leeds Polytechnic the best teaching institution in Europe.

If that seems absurdly conceited, it surprised and challenged the senior members of the academic staff when I took them away for a long weekend at a study centre in the Yorkshire Dales, to discuss and clarify the nature of a polytechnic. To those who expressed discomfort at the scale of my ambition I quoted my old Edinburgh friend George Scott-Moncrieff: 'No one is more pathetic than the man who aims low and misses.' We spent many hours arguing about what as a polytechnic we ought to be, returning constantly to the difference between a university and a polytechnic. Someone produced a couple of definitions:

a) A *university* is a collection of disparate disciplines united by a common allegiance to the central heating plant.

131

Main building of Leeds Polytechnic, new Leeds Metropolitan University, with Leeds Town Hall in background left and Leeds University in background right

b) A *polytechnic* is any institution designated as such by the Secretary of State for Education and Science.

We learned more about one another. And that was important; I had been deeply depressed at the first general meeting I held with the academic staff; some were inarticulate, one was drunk and others were frankly bored. It took me several months to discover that among them were several outstanding characters and devoted teachers. Perhaps it was part of the West Riding character to show no enthusiasm for anything.

When I took up the post, the Polytechnic (composed of four existing colleges) had a collection of buildings of varying kinds and dates. The College of Commerce was originally accommodated in a nineteenth-century building on Woodhouse Lane, which now only housed accountancy; the School of Architecture was in another building beside

132

it. Other departments of the College of Commerce were located in the centre of the city in various inadequate buildings rented by the local education authority. But the main buildings were a group just nearing completion behind the city hall. Known as the Central Colleges they had been started as a phased development in the early 1950s. The first phase contained the engineering departments for the College of Technology, the next phase most of the College of Commerce, the third phase was the Yorkshire College of Education in Home Economics and the fourth and final phase was the College of Art. It was to have been a coherent scheme with a central slab block of ten storeys and slightly lower wings spreading from it. The architects were Yorke, Rosenberg and Mardall, a prestigious and successful firm based in London and still working in many parts of the world. There had, however, been some kind of administrative crisis during the 1960s, probably caused by the College of Education in Home Economics insisting that they must have no connection with the engineers. The complex of buildings was therefore an uneven one, with half of the ten-storey slab block complete and various other blocks partially separated from it. One of my first changes was to have the home economics block linked to the others by a bridge which should have been there in the first place.

Against that background, what policy did we develop for the adaptation and use of the buildings? They were an unimpressive collection, new and old, good and bad. What were the components which would accommodate a growing polytechnic? What were the facilities that could provide some kind of unification for the Polytechnic? They had to be both social and academic. The social facilities ran by the Polytechnic were the refectories, cafés and bars (the students ran their own Students' Union). Classrooms were mostly small because of the nature of the studies and there were several types of lecture hall – some large ones in technology, a few in commerce and a small number in art.

The biggest problem was the library. At the time of the planning of the colleges, it had been expected that a large central library would occupy a major part of the site. This had been eliminated for various reasons (or excuses). Each college had its own library. The technology library was fairly adequate; the commerce library was frankly derisory (a couple of cupboards); the home economics library was good; and the art library lavish (there were two kinds of book purchase; books for the library and books for teaching, the latter being looked after by members of staff and never seen again). It was clear to me that all the libraries must be put together so that there would be one polytechnic library. After much discussion and a great deal of opposition (especially from the artists), the library became one unit with one budget.

The new buildings were bad buildings. The initial block was steel-framed with in-filling panels; the next phase had a concrete frame; the final phase was also of concrete construction with concrete slab in-filling. All of them were featureless inside, usually with separate classrooms on each side of a central corridor of standard dimensions. It was a marked contrast to the buildings of the University of York with which I was familiar.

One of my first actions was to get funds to landscape the site, with grassy mounds and several hundred trees. Some of the students dubbed these mounds 'Mount Nuttgens'. I also designed the directional signs, external and internal. We commissioned a new complex building for architecture, town planning and landscape. I had a huge sign, 'Polytechnic' erected at the top of the gable end of the central high block and set about transforming some disparate and sometimes antagonistic colleges into, I hoped, one great educational community – a community composed of many different people.

What was conspicuously lacking was any kind of social space for people to gather and talk and relax. The Student Union, opened during my first year, had some large rooms, mostly overcrowded as soon as they were opened. To create a usable social space, I took over the entrance hall of the main block and had the space furnished with armchairs available for anyone. I also designed the new enquiry counter and thus put my architectural skills to some use.

In effect, the Polytechnic was a kind of village in central Leeds. It was seriously underprivileged. The only college that had student residences was the Yorkshire College of Education in Home Economics. That had originally been the Yorkshire College of Housecraft, where girls were trained in housekeeping and catering. It had four residences at Headingly. The other colleges had no residential accommodation at all.

But now I must return to the general development and organisation of the Polytechnic. Until I moved to Leeds I had no idea how confused and ill-assorted was the organisation of education in this country. The new polytechnics had been placed in an insecure position between local and national government. They were owned by local authorities, but had remits which were national in character. All the parties concerned with their administration and funding were able to frustrate things; few were able to exercise any real authority.

In that, Leeds Polytechnic was no different from the others, but it suffered from a special and fundamental problem, which I had not appreciated before arriving but soon did. This was the direct consequence of the City Council's decision to keep a firm control over the Polytechnic by putting the approval of its work under two separate committees of the Council – the academic side under education and the non-academic staff (administrative, secretarial and technical) under establishment. This led to a grotesque imbalance in the planning of the personnel of the Polytechnic. But that, as I soon began to appreciate, was a harsh reality which manifested itself in the insecurity of many academic and administrative staff – and was of course aggravated by the inadequacy of the financial provision.

What I did not appreciate for many years – until in fact nearly the end of the decade at the start of which the Polytechnic was founded – was how bitterly some of the members and officials of the local authority resented us and wished to damage us. I felt as if I was trying to lead a charge in a military campaign while the general staff far behind were trying to shoot us. I think the best way to explain that is by including in this story a particularly distressing event which I later described in an article in *The Times Higher Education Supplement*, for which I wrote a weekly column from 1979 to 1987.

About the middle of July 1979 rumours began to spread through Leeds that corruption of some kind was rife in the Polytechnic. They were supported by reports in the local evening paper, *The Yorkshire Evening Post* by the correspondent who handled local authority meetings and issues. It was clear that the rumours emanated from the City Council.

In the last week of July, I had a meeting with the Chief Officer of the Corporation and the Director of Finance. I was accompanied by Gordon Wright, the Deputy Director of the Polytechnic responsible for its financial affairs. It was accepted that an investigation was indeed being carried out, at the request of the leader of the City Council, Councillor Sparling. It was not however possible to let us know what was being investigated. The Director of Finance offered to complete his investigation by the end of the week and meet us again. It was submitted to the leader of the Council, who referred it to the police. He did more; he held a press conference which resulted in a report in *The Yorkshire Evening Post* under the heading 'Poly: Police Called In'. It reported that the police had been called in 'to investigate alleged irregularities over building contracts, worth hundreds of thousands of pounds, for work at Leeds Polytechnic'. The Director of Finance informed me that since the matter was now in the hands of the police he could not after all tell me what it was about or who was involved.

We seemed to be getting involved in the nightmarish secrecy of a police state. I called in my own lawyer, at my own expense, to help me to find out what was happening. The damage to the Polytechnic was serious. Rumours and suspicions had been inflamed by press reports and the local authority grapevine. Accompanied by police officers, members of the audit section of the authority had entered offices and taken away files – all the files of the Maintenance Officer since April 1977, various files from the Deputy and Assistant Directors and one letter from my own files of 1970, setting out the duties of the Maintenance Officer, as well as files from the offices of three contractors who had done work for the Polytechnic. The report in the evening paper and the confiscation of the files indicated that the problem concerned building contracts. They could not be major ones such as the new Brunswick Building because that was being handled by the city architect; nor could they involve hundreds of thousands of pounds because the Maintenance Officer handled no such contracts.

There the matter rested, as far as official relationships were concerned, for a year and a half, until April 1981, when the police reported to the City Council that nothing criminal had occurred and that no action was to be taken. The Council did not pass on the information to me; I had to find it out for myself and have it confirmed, which the Director of Finance did in a letter of notable ill grace.

The matter had not of course rested there for the Polytechnic and particularly for the members of staff who had been under suspicion. The demoralisation of the maintenance staff was for a time almost complete. The personal agony of individuals, whom I knew could not possibly have engaged in anything like the crimes being investigated and talked about, was incalculable.

What had actually happened? The allegations centred upon contracts for minor works and maintenance and revealed the undisguised informality of our procedures for getting such work carried out. We had not flouted but manipulated the articles of Government of the polytechnic so as to carry out the work with an inadequate number of staff, at reasonable speed and at considerably less cost than would have been incurred had we followed all the official procedures rigidly. The coincidence of first myself and later an Assistant Director being architects meant that we could

137

(at whatever cost to ourselves in overwork) carry out a lot of architectural functions, including surveys of buildings, brief specifications of work and supervision on the site, at no cost to the authority. With help from members of academic staff qualified in surveying and costing, we could confirm that the jobs were reasonably priced. We knew for example that the work of bringing the main libraries together on three floors of the central building had been estimated by the city architect as needing £65,000 and that we had done it with our maintenance staff and local small contractors for £22,000. In the same way many of the houses we used in Queen Square had been restored and adapted entirely out of the Polytechnic's maintenance budget and without more than a few sketch drawings. On a conservative estimate we had saved the corporation at least £100,000 and probably much more.

The story I have been recounting was not, I suspect, unique. In calling in the police without consulting me as the head of the institution concerned, the leader of the Council was, I learned, behaving in a manner normal in a local authority, however indecent such practice might seem to an outside observer. But the Polytechnic was not a standard corporation department but a semi-autonomous body owned by the Council but working within carefully defined articles of Government. The behaviour of some of the officials and several elected members seemed to me indefensible and the failure even to consult the head of the institution revealed a capacity for loyalty and honour that deserved a place in the annals of political squalor.

Local authorities are notoriously vulnerable to corruption. I wondered what – and in which part of the authority – corruption had actually occurred. As he left my room after confiscating a few files, the Inspector from the Fraud Squad suggested quietly that if I wanted to know how rumours about polytechnic corruption got into the local evening paper I should drop into a certain bar on a certain day of the week. I took his advice and watched councillors, and the leader of the Council, exchanging gossip with local

Allerton Park, a Victorian Country House, drawn when leased by
Leeds Polytechnic for short courses

139

journalists. Within a few days my grapevine told me how alarmed they had been by my presence. For my part, I realised that I should have known more about local politics and how policies are decided.

That was a temporary setback. But I never ceased to ask: where was the Polytechnic going? There was always a certain tension between academic respectability and devotion to the world of work. What came to be known as 'academic drift' was the easy acceptance of academic respectability. But we were trying to do something more serious, and more difficult. For I believed we were engaged in a major educational revolution.

If there was to be a serious change – in the direction of usefulness, of jobs, of activity, of work – the polytechnics had to be not just second-choice institutions but the key to the future. In other words, vocational education and training (to the highest possible level) must be as estimable as – and more urgently needed than – the conventional studies that are regarded as having higher status. A production engineer or an industrial engineer must be regarded with every bit as much respect, and educated with every bit as much care, as a specialist in English literature, a philosopher, a researcher in chemistry or an historian. But that had not happened since the early nineteenth century. We needed, I thought, more of the oil can and less of the inkwell.

So it was important that we teach the right things and try to establish the right way to teach them. The right things were not 'subjects' or 'disciplines', the conventional divisions of learning which make it easy to teach the same subjects indefinitely, but *activities*, learning to *do* something. To take two simple examples, we must teach people to speak and use a foreign language in daily intercourse, both private and commercial, not just learn about foreign literature; we must train people to be social workers, not just study sociology. We must teach people skills, not just the ability to appreciate and criticise.

This approach affected the provision of facilities within the Polytechnic buildings. For our teaching must be conducted in workshops, studios and laboratories as much as in classrooms; our library must not be just storage for the products of past minds, but a resource centre providing access to necessary information, methods and materials. The general orientation of our studies had to be *action*; it might be pursued by what came to be known as *action learning*. A polytechnic, I decided, using its correct meaning as a guide, was an institution (and eventually a community) for the development and teaching of the practical arts. That required qualities such as clarity of mind, decisiveness, the ability to work together in groups, practical and manual skills and an understanding of physical reality. The future of our most successful and brilliant graduates would be not to continue in the institution, like a professor in a university, but to leave it and become deeply involved in the world of practical affairs.

These considerations confirmed my earlier view that a polytechnic should concentrate on *teaching* rather than *research*. It is impossible to escape the dominance of research in universities and the role it plays nowadays in the academic ethos and funding. In the early days of the Polytechnic, I used to make light-hearted remarks in speeches to the effect that what many universities called 'research' we might in the Polytechnic call 'reading books', 'working in the lab or studio', or even simply 'keeping up with my subject'. These were activities I expected of myself and my staff, not just so that they could bring glory on themselves and the Polytechnic by publishing or acquiring postgraduate degrees, but because they were essential if we were continually to improve the quality of our teaching. With this end in view, I set up the Educational Technology Unit as a service unit helping to improve, and if necessary transform, the standard of teaching so that we would become the best *teaching* institution in the country.

What extended the work of the Polytechnic and made the emphasis on teaching even more significant was the decision of central Government (realised by the local authority) to close some of the teacher training colleges and amalgamate

Leeds Polytechnic
BECKETT PARK
Patrick Nuttgens 1976

JAMES GRAHAM COLLEGE
Patrick Nuttgens 1976

HAMMOND HOUSE
Leeds Polytechnic
Patrick Nuttgens 1976

Edward Heath drawn on the back of my invitation card

others with the Polytechnic. I received my first intimation of this when I attended a dinner in 1973 at 10 Downing Street at the invitation of Edward Heath as Prime Minister, called by him to discuss the future of higher education and attended by about ten Vice-Chancellors and three or four polytechnic directors. I was one of them. In the discussion which followed dinner, the senior civil servant in education, Bill Pile (later Sir William Pile) predicted that by 1980 we would be producing twice as many graduates as there would be jobs available of the kind which graduates expected to obtain. Second, there would be nearly 1 million fewer children in the schools in 1980 than had been planned for in 1970. Some schools would therefore contract and fewer new ones would be built; there must also be a reduction in the number of students being trained for teaching.

Mrs Thatcher, as Secretary of State for Education, was co-host at that dinner in Downing Stret. Her White Paper *Education: A Framework for Expansion* was published in 1973. In fact it was a framework for contraction. And that for a good reason. It was at last recognised by the Government that the birth rate had, in fact, been dropping since 1965, and that there would not be enough pupils to fill all the schools and require the staff who were already trained or about to be trained by the colleges of education. The solution to this was at first muddled and confused and, in many ways, unsatisfactory. What it meant in practice for us was that the teacher training colleges in Leeds (with the exception of the department in the University) were amalgamated with the Polytechnic which now became a larger and more comprehensive organisation – still geared to courses aimed at vocations (one of which was teacher training), but wider in its scope and infinitely more complex in the motives of its students and in popular esteem.

Teacher training brings to a head many of the problems of higher education because it is the link between schools of all levels and higher education at all levels. In the great expansion of the 1960s the teacher training colleges had tried to become mini-universities. They became colleges of *education* and shrank away from their original title of *training*. Because of the organisation of subjects in the schools along traditional lines (English, history, geography, physics, chemistry, biology, etc.) it seemed logical to organise their teacher training colleges along the same lines with a little training in teaching methods and more in the history and theory of education. Because of that and because, in any case, their courses were validated by the universities, they followed a pattern which was in effect a reflection of the universities.

The joining of the teacher training colleges with the polytechnics meant, in the case of those polytechnics which thought the matter through, a fundamental revolution in

144

their way of thinking. If the teacher training section was to draw upon the polytechnic's expertise as a whole, and if its students were to become part of the community of learning for work, it followed that the courses and the areas of expertise in which the future schoolteachers were trained were unlikely to be exactly the same as those of the former colleges and the existing universities.

But that meant that the teachers likely to be produced by a polytechnic school of education might not be exactly matched to the conventional needs of the schools. Was it likely that the needs of the schools would change? It seemed to me essential that they should change – and essential precisely because schools were (by political decision) becoming comprehensive. If comprehensive schooling was to mean anything other than a political flag, it must be because the schools would sooner or later see their way to establishing, at the same levels as the more conventional academic studies, work and activities for the boys and girls in the school which would lead them directly and meaning-fully into the world of work. That, it seemed to me, was where the enlarged polytechnics should belong.

Of course, it was not as simple as that. The polytechnics were part of a minority provision, catering for the less than 20 per cent of school-leavers who at that time went on to higher education. If the polytechnics were to offer, as they theoretically did, an alternative to the universities, they must offer an education and training that was wider than that of the universities. They should be genuinely compre-hensive. At least they should be essential components of a system of higher education, able to meet the needs of the boys and girls coming to the polytechnic from comprehen-sive schools. That would only make sense if higher edu-cation were seen to be comprehensive at its own level. Polytechnics, like the majority of schools, must be con-cerned with action, with training people for work in its widest sense, with the world (and the culture) of doing and making.

We were a happy team. Among the outstanding teachers

and organisers of teaching was Hubert Eichinger, head of the Modern Languages Centre (at first in Harrogate Road and later, when we took over the teacher training colleges, in the former James Graham College at Farnley). He was responsible for an activity (learning languages for use in business and government as well as holidays) that seemed to me exactly what a polytechnic ought to be doing. The Modern Languages Centre was more than a study centre; it was the most lively place for people of all ages and nationalities gathering for learning and fun.

As local centres for part-time as well as full-time students, the constituent colleges did not have the carers that one would expect to find in a university. The Bishop of Ripon asked me to appoint a chaplain; we found an admirable lady who worked closely with the University chaplain. The Polytechnic was essentially a secular body; I therefore made no special arrangements for Catholic students even though I was a Catholic myself. But I worked closely with the Catholic Chaplain in the University (at first Fr Alban Byron and then Fr Rory Geoghegan, both Jesuits). More immediately helpful was a psychiatric social worker, Monty Quate, whom we recruited as Student Counsellor. Like many other such professionals he found himself counselling academic staff as much as students. Despite the local authority's characteristically grudging response to our request, we appointed a nurse and modified a building to form a dispensary.

And finally there were the drivers. From some mistaken wish to be as economical as possible, I never claimed expenses for driving my own car; but as soon as possible we bought an estate car for the Polytechnic. The parsimonious local authority refused for a long time to replace it when it was worn out. This resulted in an absurd situation. After I was awarded a CBE, the letters were proudly stencilled after my name on the side of the car – immediately below a hole of about three inches across. But I was driven everywhere by two drivers. Sid Green took me to Buckingham Palace when I was given a CBE. The regular driver, Alan

Jerusalem 1979 at the Western Wall

147

Wonnacott, took us to Windsor Castle when Biddy and I stayed there for a night as guests of the Queen. Alan took me everywhere – to London and Bristol and Plymouth and Scotland – he looked after me when I became disabled and became a close and much loved friend. There are few companionships more close and valuable than that of two people in a car. When he wasn't driving me he took books to and from the National Lending Library at Thorp Arch.

But at the beginning and end – especially after I became seriously disabled – I depended on my inexhaustible and perceptive secretary, Anne Fairburn. An exceptionally amusing student leader wrote a regular column in the student paper, inspired by a similarly named column in *Private Eye*, supposed to be letters written by me to her every week. They were entitled 'Dear Anne'. The phrase is appropriate for the conclusion to this part of my account.

I left the Polytechnic in 1986 believing that we had not only established a reputable educational institution in Leeds but played a significant part in defining the polytechnic ethos for the country and (I hoped) a much wider cultural environment. We had joined a European and wider world of social and technical and artistic development. It did not occur to me that the polytechnic ethos would be quickly destroyed.

The death of the polytechnic was not a natural demise; it was a deliberate execution. It occurred in two phases. In April 1989 the polytechnics were taken away from the local authorities and became independent. That could only be beneficial and relieved them of many of the frustrations that made it difficult to be a coherent institution. It had seemed to me an admirable idea to combine advanced education and training with the education of everyone.

Then, in September 1992 the polytechnics were renamed universities. Some of them were sufficiently proud and intellectually secure to wish to keep the name 'polytechnic.' But the national mood was against it and had I remained in the Polytechnic, I would have had to accept that effectively all the parents in this class-conscious country hoped that their children would go to a university. The Conservative Government was able furthermore to claim that it had hugely expanded higher education and doubled the number of universities merely by changing the name of the institutions. Leeds Polytechnic became Leeds Metropolitan University.

But let me return to my own story and that of the growing family. I had been head-hunted for the jobs I had done. I was now approached for many others and usually failed to get them. Two universities interviewed me as a possible Vice-Chancellor, two Oxford colleges invited me to discuss their masterships, Edinburgh College of Art approached me for its Headship (I refused). I was persuaded by a celebrated governor to apply to be Rector of the Royal College of Art on two occasions (and just missed it) and (for once) I applied for the Vice-Chancellorship of the Open University which seemed appropriate for me – and did not even reach the short list. I chaired several Advisory Councils for the BBC and, increasingly, bodies concerned with disability.

But any such failures did not depress us. We always had a good house and came to love Yorkshire. At first when I took the job in Leeds, we did not need to move house; we stayed in the village of Clifford. Then with the amalgamation of the Polytechnic with the colleges of education, a house for the Director became available on the site of the City of Leeds College at Beckett Park. We moved there in 1976 to the best house we ever made our own. Sheltered on two sites by thick belts of trees – we woke to the dawn chorus of innumerable birds – and on the others by well-kept lawns and tennis courts, the house was a simple two-storey brick building of 1912, originally the Vice-Principal's house and then the Principal's when his absurdly large residence was converted for students. It was light and spacious.

And I made it a superb family home. I adjusted the ground floor rooms so that the living and dining and study spaces could be opened into one very large room for receptions, and the kitchen was furnished with a huge central table so that it became a family room, constantly crowded with our own children and many friends. It seemed like a re-creation of the home for living and working that I had always wanted.

We sold the house in Clifford and bought an elegant holiday house in Coverdale, to which we would have eventually retired had not my increasing disability made it inaccessible. Between the two houses and many travels our lives were varied and stimulating – and active.

From what I have written so far it might be concluded that the Polytechnic and its fortunes occupied the whole of my life. It certainly dominated it. But there was another dimension both within and without my official employment. Among many other activities, I reviewed regularly for various journals. But most of my journalism was for *The Times Higher Education Supplement*, for which between 1979 and 1987 I must have written at least 200 articles and columns. In December 1979 the editor of that supplement, Brian MacArthur, commissioned a monthly feature article on themes chosen by me and not confined to higher or indeed any level of education. I wrote more than fifty articles. Then, at the end of August 1984 his successor, Peter Scott, commissioned a weekly column, shorter than the articles, under the title 'Fifth Column', as free in choice of subject as the title implies. It was for me perpetually stimulating, wide ranging and often entertaining. I continued writing until the end of December 1987 when I set out to different parts of the country, filming for my BBC series on housing, *The Home Front*. That was the end of my regular writing. It was also the last serious broadcasting I did after so many years of involvement with the BBC.

Not only broadcasting and writing. Shortly after joining the Polytechnic, I became involved with so many outside activities that my time was constantly taken up with travelling to and from other places. In January 1971 I was in London twice, once chairing the RIBA Books Committee

150

and once attending the BBC's General Advisory Council. In the next five years I lectured in Birmingham, Warrington and Sheffield. In one year I made broadcasts from London, attended polytechnic meetings at Coombe Lodge in Gloucestershire and at the BBC's Senior Management Conference Centre in Buckinghamshire. I spoke in Manchester, made a television programme in London, spoke at the Scottish Georgian Society's AGM, at a town planning conference at the Preservation Trust in St Andrews and at a conference on the future of polytechnics in London. Lectures and meetings took me in quick sucession to London, Newcastle, Manchester, Edinburgh, Bath, Windsor, Durham, Oxford, Cambridge, Glasgow and Aberdeen. I attended conferences in Lincoln, Bristol and Hull, broadcast from Canterbury and Plymouth, and attended meetings in Manchester, Doncaster, Salford and York.

Some of these lectures were specially related to my own background and expertise. At the 400th anniversary celebration at the University of Edinburgh, I lectured about the University's teaching of Technology. At an international conference on Crafts in Vienna, I surveyed the development of crafts in Britain and discussed education and training. Then I took a major part in an international conference on Design at Aspen in Colorado. I delivered the keynote address on the history of Design in the United Kingdom, took part in its discussions and gave the final summary, receiving a standing ovation as the conference drew to a close.

But the most unexpected and memorable of all my activities were events that were external to the Polytechnic but must have been caused by my part in it. In 1976, for example, I received an invitation from the US State Department to spend a month in the United States following an agreed route after a week in Washington. My wife accompanied me for most of the journey, from Washington and Virginia to Santa Fé and then Arizona and California and finally Chicago. We visited universities and art galleries and concert halls and museums, and I seized the opportunity to

151

see many of the great modern buildings of America. In particular I visited buildings by Frank Lloyd Wright which are essential to an understanding of the modern movement in architecture – especially Taliesin West near Phoenix and the houses in Oak Park, Chicago.

While in Los Angeles I received a telegram inviting me to luncheon in Buckingham Palace. Soon after my return I therefore hurried to the Palace with another seven guests and was suitably impressed, not only by the Queen and the Duke of Edinburgh but by the sheer efficiency and impeccable timing of a relaxed informal meal. That superb organisation was even more evident a few years later when Biddy and I stayed a night at Windsor Castle, had a delightful dinner and were given a guided tour of the royal apartments by the Queen and the Duke.

Those were not the only special episodes. In 1983 we spent a month in Australia at the invitation of its Education Department, lecturing in colleges of education and universities, mainly about the reorganisation of higher education in Great Britain but also (whenever I had the chance) about architecture, especially the great architects of the turn of the century. And I spent several days exploring the various components of Sydney Opera House and decided that it reaffirmed modern architecture as one of the great original movements in the discipline's history.

Especially fascinating was a visit to South Korea in 1973 to lecture at a huge international conference on 'Innovation to Higher Education'. My paper, translated into Korean, was about the invention and development – and thus the philosophy – of the polytechnics. We were welcomed and entertained by a Prime Minister/President. I visited the border with North Korea at Panmunjom and seized the opportunity to visit universities and colleges.

But in many ways the most memorable episode was the previously mentioned dinner at 10 Downing Street of university Vice-Chancellors and polytechnic Directors, hosted by Edward Heath as Prime Minister and Margaret Thatcher as Secretary of State for Education. As a result of a lively conversation with Mr Heath, I was given a guided tour of the house by him after the dinner. A year later his party lost the election and Mrs Thatcher replaced Heath as leader of the party. She became Prime Minister at the election in 1979. Heath's demotion was sad, and I thought undeserved. But not unexpected. An opaque, brilliant, capable but strangely uncommunicating man.

The lectures continued, in many parts of the country. For example, the Director of Crown Paints organised what was called 'The Colour Lecture', which I inaugurated at Manchester University and then delivered, refined and repeated in many other cities. Helped and organised by the most capable and reliable secretary any senior academic has ever had (Anne Fairburn), I was constantly on the move, constantly (I hope) publicising Leeds Polytechnic and all polytechnics by demonstrating how well we could present material and widen the scope of higher education.

But while my intellectual and social life was blooming, the same could not be said of my physical condition. The effect of my illnesses – especially the poliomyelitis from which I had suffered during my schooldays – was having an increasing effect and becoming more obvious. The long-term effects of polio became known as 'post-polio syndrome'. The characteristics of it were that the part of one's anatomy left damaged by polio became progressively worse while the undamaged parts were grossly overworked to compensate, and themselves became worn out. I spent a few weeks in the Nuffield Hospital in Oxford. But the serious nature of my disability only became obvious to me when I applied to be the Head of a new polytechnic in Hong Kong. There is no doubt that the job would have been mine had not both the appointment committee and I myself insisted on a medical examination. The report from the doctor stated unequivocally that I was not fit for the job. At about the same time, I was diagnosed by a consultant physician in Leeds as having not just the results of polio but multiple sclerosis. The treatments for the two diseases were diametrically opposed, for if it was possible to overcome the effects of polio by 'constantly challenging one's muscles', it was only possible to cope with MS by never becoming tired and making great precautions in terms of physical exercise. I had already taken to the use of a simple motorised wheelchair, whose appearance in the Polytechnic corridors always provoked amusement and friendly concern.

In 1986 I took early retirement from the Polytechnic and (without intending to do so) started another career. The University of York offered me an honorary Professorship and awarded me an honorary Doctorate. Within a year, I picked up four honorary Doctorates – from York, Sheffield, the Open University and the Heriod Watt at Edinburgh, and later from what became Leeds Metropolitan University. I shared a room in the King's Manor (the Institute of Advanced Architectural Studies) and wrote several books.

I had already, whilst at Leeds, produced three books on the history of architecture. One was a coffee table book on world architecture. Another was intended to be a companion volume to Gombrich's *Story of Art*. It was entitled *The Story of Architecture* and dealt with the history of architecture from the pyramids to the present day. It was publisheed by Phaidon and was issued in both a hard- and paperback edition. I decided to employ Biddy as my researcher; she decided to write it instead. Most of the book is by her except for the opening chapters, anything on vernacular architecture, the chapter on mediaeval Europe and all the chapters from the beginning of the nineteenth century to the present day. A second, and larger, edition was produced in 1997, fully revised and brilliantly illustrated. In my view (of course), it is the best book on world architecture now available.

More difficult to produce was the pocket-sized Mitchell Beazley *Guide to Architecture* on which I employed several of my family. Biddy wrote in 100 words the entire geography, geology, history and politics of the period and our son Nicholas roughed out the notes on the buildings. It is literally a pocket guide which covers everything from the first civilisations to the postmodern period, thoroughly illus-

154

trated with line drawings by a variety of artists. At the same time, my book on York, *York, the Continuing City*, was republished by Maxiprint in York with new coloured photographs by John Shannon, Chairman of York Civic Trust.

More challenging was the book commissioned by Unwin Hyman on modern architecture, entitled *Understanding Modern Architecture*. I had given a series of lectures at Leeds University under the title 'The Architecture of Pluralism'. I believe that was a more accurate title than 'Understanding Modern Architecture'. All the copies were sold. More complex was the book I wrote (with the help from a postgraduate student at the University of York) to accompany a series of television programmes I made on social housing. *The Home Front* had a subtitle 'Housing the People 1840–1990'. The six programmes made seven chapters. We filmed throughout England and Scotland from Glasgow to Plymouth and including Northern Ireland, where the Northern Ireland Housing Executive had produced some of the best social housing of the post-war years.

Despite all these activities I had never ceased sketching and making watercolours, taking with me a sketchbook on all my journeys and especially during vacations. As the intellectual and organisational demands of the Polytechnic became all-absorbing, I began to describe my vocational artistic productions as a form of psychotherapy. Much of the work was produced in Scotland where we spent many weeks as guests of Harry Jefferson Barnes, the Director of Glasgow School of Art, who had been a key figure in the formation of the Charles Rennie Mackintosh Society, of which I became a Vice-President.

But painting in Scotland became for me more serious as a result of a wretched episode during my time in Leeds. A senior figure in arts features at the BBC, John Drummond, consulted me for many months on a possible series of TV programmes on the architecture of Great Britain and then commissioned me, not to present them, but to write them. I made all the necessary arrangements, including three sabbatical terms at suitable intervals. I was about to sign the contract when he cancelled my involvement. He had by then picked my brains sufficiently to choose a number of author-presenters for specialised periods under the title *The Spirit of the Age*. I wrote and presented the programme on the Arts and Crafts Movement.

With a summer term thus made free, I drove with our second son Jamie around the west and north coasts of Scotland, drawing and painting every day and gradually clearing my mind of the anger and frustration I felt after such an experience. Drummond later became Artistic Director of the Edinburgh Festival and then returned to a senior post in the BBC and a knighthood.

My career as a broadcaster and presenter of TV programmes came to an end with the series on housing and a few local programmes. What did not come to an end was what had started as a private occupation and what I described as my own psychotherapy. That was painting, at first in oils and, when that became impossible with my increasing disability, exclusively in watercolours. I exhibited from time to time and finally had two exhibitions of my own work, one in Coxwold and one in York. As I write this, I am still sketching and painting.

The family dispersed, though not as widely as Biddy's family which, in a truly Scottish tradition are to be found in many distant parts of the world. Our children either stayed in Leeds and its environs or moved to London. What I had not expected was that many of them became addicted to the media and found employment therein. Of the five boys and three girls, Nicholas, James, Giles, Susie and Sandy either work in the theatre, produce and make films, make music, or broadcast. Our foster-son Kurt trained as a butcher and then founded his own business supplying and selling milk.

For me, one of the serious social developments was the succession of friendships with members of the clergy, not only Catholics but increasingly Anglicans. At Clifford we had always taken part in the activities of its Catholic church; in Leeds I became close friends with successive Vicars of

156

the parish church and especially the parish church of St Chad at Headingley. The Master of Music at Leeds parish church, Simon Lindley, became a member of staff at the Polytechnic and since leaving it has remained a close friend.

On that note I end this story. My confidence in politicians was never great but in the representatives of the churches I discovered meanings that were often profound if never uncritical. Theology is as much a cause of division and hatred as nationalism and greed. The message of Christ – that we should all be one and united in love – has been rejected throughout history. In the year that records the two-thousandth anniversary of his birth, I finish my story hoping that in a small and local way I have not increased those divisions but taken part in mutual activities and possibly helped fellow students of life and learning to find themselves and contribute to our culure and happiness.

Gregory steering the barge on the Oxford Canal

APPENDIX: THE PHILOSOPHY OF POLYTECHNIC EDUCATION

Throughout all the changes and innovations for which I was responsible at Leeds, there always remained for me a fundamental question, to which as an experienced academic I was constantly hoping to find an answer: what is the *idea* of a polytechnic?

University people might ask, what is a polytechnic? I would reply that universities had had several centuries to decide what was a university and were still arguing. We should be allowed at least ten years to find our answer. I set about lecturing on the subject, writing articles and finally a book called *What Should We Teach and How Should We Teach It?*

Before assembling that book I had built up some powerful arguments. The Society of Industrial Artists and Designers offered me an award, The Burton Award, to prepare a paper (and lecture) on Design. I spent a summer at my father's studio and wrote an extended lecture entitled 'Learning to Some Purpose'. A year later I gave the first in a series of annual lectures sponsored by Stanley Tools, entitled 'Living and Learning in the World of Work'. In thinking about both papers I reread A. N. Whitehead's *The Aims of Education and Other Essays* and applied some of his fundamental philosophical principles to my own argument. I backed them up by studying two books by the philosopher under whom I had studied in Edinburgh, John MacMurray: *The Self as Agent* and *Persons in Relation*.

I occasionally described my conclusions as a philosophy of polytechnic education and training and append it here as a more detailed account of the conclusions reached so far in my book.

In the 150 years following the Industrial Revolution we had contrived to create an educational system that had failed to respond to the actual needs of society, of industry and the professions. To understand that, and to find a key to our present problems, it seemed to me essential to look at that tradition, at the beliefs and values established in the nineteenth century and the response of the educational establishment to the Industrial Revolution and its aftermath.

In a succession of lectures and articles in journals I insisted on the impossibility of discussing the educational system of today without recognising the fundamental changes to intellectual and personal horizons made by the Industrial Revolution and its aftermath. The fact that, at least in principle, we are no longer concerned with education and training for a minority but with education and training for everyone is a fundamental aspect of the Industrial Revolution and the urban revolution that accompanied it. Those movements opened up huge new areas of work, new possibilities for invention and design, new sources of power. They demanded new skills and new aspirations. And they threw into prominence new people.

They came from all sorts of backgrounds, geographical and social, and were various in character and attainment. But they did have this in common – that, by and large, the pioneers of the new processes that made the Industrial Revolution possible were not distinguished by their education. The Arkwrights, Brindley, Telford, Stephenson and other innovators in the field of education itself managed brilliantly despite that conspicuous disadvantage. It may even be that their lack of formal (and certainly any kind of higher) education was a benefit. They could look at a problem directly, assess it without preconceptions, devise original ways of solving it, create artefacts without aesthetic prejudice and call upon new skills, usually at first without training.

The schools gradually set up to provide that training were essentially practical and based upon work – not upon an appreciation of what it might be like to work, but as an aid to people already doing work. The first Mechanics' Institutes were set up in the 1820s. Between then and the Technical Instruction Act of 1889, they had mixed fortunes and many discouragements, in notable contrast with their equivalents on the continent. During their halting development into colleges and institutes of technology and art they were part-time and often evening schools, where people from work could more conveniently be taught (by experienced people also from work) the skills that they needed and others that they might need for the future. That is not to describe an ideal system to be reviewed with nostalgia; it is merely to point to an important characteristic of practical education: that the best way to learn a thing is to do it.

A convenient moment at which to appreciate what happened in England is 1851. In that year, the Great Exhibition brought people, both visitors and observers and industrial entrepreneurs from all over the world to see in the Exhibition (and in the industrial cities) not only the peculiarities of contemporary Victorian taste but the practical effects of the Industrial Revolution that Britain had pioneered. It was a fitting culmination to a century of invention and change – for the 100 years from 1750 to 1850 were the most formative period of the Industrial Revolution, starting in the hills and valleys of Britain, spreading to Europe and ultimately affecting the whole world.

The visitors to the Great Exhibition did not just look with wonder; they studied what had happened and took the knowledge back to their own countries to develop processes most of which had been initiated in Great Britain. They did so just as this country was doing its best to turn its back upon the very discoveries and processes that had made it the crucible of a new age. The Europeans not only followed the new processes; they took a hard look at the way people

160

were being trained to use them. And having already initiated a system of education relevant to the needs of industrial society, they elaborated it. Two years after the exhibition, Dr Lyon Playfair, having studied industrial education in Europe, reported that European industry was bound to overtake Britain if Britain failed to alter its outlook and methods.

The European countries had every reason to proceed with confidence. In contrast to our halting and never full-blooded attempts to set up a few classes in technical instruction (with the Mechanics' Institutes, some part-time studies and eventually local colleges of technology) the European countries had already been establishing powerful places of learning and instruction, serious institutions for the study and practice of technology at the highest level.

The French *École Polytechnique*, still one of the most prestigious centres of education in Europe, was founded in 1794. It should be noted that it was set up to train not only key administrators but also skilled experts in engineering and public works; and it was accompanied by a new *Conservatoire des Arts et Metiers*. The *Polytechnische Institut* of Vienna was founded in 1815; the *Technische Hochschule* at Karlsruhe in 1825; the schools at Dresden in 1828 and Stuttgart in 1829. It took until 1890 before they could grant their own degrees but by 1851 they were already institutions of senior rank. The most celebrated of the polytechnics in Europe was the *Zurich Polytecknikum* founded in 1855. That influenced Germany in particular and it was Germany that influenced America. In America, the *Massachusetts Institute of Technology* was founded in 1865.

It is significant that in every country in which technical education was taken seriously its development was accompanied by a system of national education – a recognition of the elementary fact that if they were to play a part in the changing world *everyone* must have instruction in reading and writing and counting. The contrast with England was many times recorded and equally often ignored. After Britain's disastrously poor performance at the Paris Exhibition of 1867, Dr Lyon Playfair wrote, in a letter quoted in *The Times*:

> Deficient representation in some of the industries might have accounted for this judgement against us, but when we find that out of 90 classes there are scarcely a dozen in which pre-eminence is unhesitatingly awarded to us, this plea must be abandoned . . . So far as I could gather them by conversation, the one cause upon which there was most unanimity of conviction is that France, Prussia, Austria, Belgium and Switzerland possess good systems of industrial education for the masters and managers of factories and workshops, and that England possesses none.

It was not only Lyon Playfair who viewed the situation with dismay. Thirty years later, the Royal Commission on Technical Education of 1884 emphasised the superiority of German over English school education and the general level of ignorance in England among working people. Forster's Educaton Act of 1870 had made it possible for money to be provided out of the rates to set up new schools, and in 1880 primary education became compulsory. But it was not until 1902 that the new Education Act initiated a coherent system of state secondary education. Even after that it was many years before the majority of children stayed at school beyond the age of fourteen.

In the technical field, the Technical Instruction Act of 1889 authorised local authorities to use for technical education the produce of a penny rate. There were a few technical colleges, a handful of polytechnics in London, a few exceptions in the North of England like the colleges of the 1870s to 1890s which were in the early 1900s to become the great civic universities of Manchester, Leeds and Liverpool. The Imperial College of Science and Technology was founded in 1903. But apart from that there were in the early years of the twentieth century only thirty-one technical schools, with fewer than 3,000 students between them. Of the universities, only Edinburgh indulged in a brief flirtation with technology with the appointment of George Wilson, a remarkable man qualified in both medicine and chemistry, to a Chair of Technology in 1855. He was the first and last holder of the Chair.

Looking at the situation dispassionately, it must be concluded that the reluctance of Britain to develop a coherent system of technical education rested upon a deeply-rooted dislike of technology, and therefore of the developing world. The attitude of the people developing the education system was not to exploit that world but in some way to escape from it, to provide answers to it. In that sense it was a development not of excitement and wonder but of fear.

In the light of the history of this country, it is all the more extraordinary that this should have happened. It was not, I believe, the result of something inherent in the national character but a direct reponse, by the intelligentsia, the professors, the clergy and the gentry to the urgent and demanding world of the Industrial Revolution. It should, after all, have been easy to build upon the fascination with science of the seventeenth century, the spirit of the founders of the Royal Society, the conviction that men were becoming the masters and possessors of nature; or upon the Enlightenment of the eighteenth century when men of genius, in Whitehead's words, 'applied the seventeenth-century group of scientific abstractions to the analysis of the unbounded universe'. In the event, that excitement became more rarefied, and distinct from the everyday world of technological change. And the mainstream of the intellectual world moved away from the industrial world altogether. It was at heart a retreat – a retreat from reality. And it found its shelter, appropriately, in the cloisters of Oxford.

Three figures of nineteenth-century Oxford will suffice as representative of that education ethos. Mark Pattison is usually accepted as the prototype for Mr Casaubon, the pedant in George Eliot's *Middlemarch*. In fact, Pattison swung between pedantry and a revival of standards of scholarship and teaching at a time when Oxford was badly in need of it. But he remains a symbol – almost the type – of academic scholarship and personal remoteness, obsessed with and utterly absorbed by the minutiae of the intellectual life.

More creatively, John Henry Newman (Cardinal Newman) represents – and in his *Idea of a University* specifically set out – ideals of university education, and thus of education as a whole. Central to his approach was the idea of education as an end in itself, untouched at its highest and best by having to make things or earn a living:

> The process of training, by which the intellect, instead of being formed or sacrificed to some particular or accidental purpose, some specific trade or profession, or study or science, is disciplined for its own sake, for the perception of its own proper object, and for its own higher culture, is called liberal education; and though there is no one in whom it is carried as far as is conceivable, or whose intellect would be a pattern of what intellects should be made, yet there is scarcely anyone but may gain an idea of what real training is, and at least look towards it and make its true scope and result, not something else, his standard of excellence; and numbers there are who may submit themselves to it, and secure it to themselves in good measure. And to set forth the right standard, and to train according to it, and to help forward all students towards it according to their various capabilities, this I conceive to be the business of a university.

This is a sentiment wholly admirable and appropriate for its time. To us, looking back at the situation now, it seems that Newman was more precisely reflecting the irony of his time than he himself imagined. For he wrote at a critical moment when the impact of the Industrial Revolution was transforming society. To him the answer to that problem lay in a liberal education. But it involved withdrawing from the ordinary, unacceptable, degrading environment of work that the Industrial Revolution was producing. As the population crowded into monstrous cities and multiplied, the life of the mind was seen to withdraw to the attractive, leisurely and genteel surroundings of Oxford and Cambridge. A university education became again what it has always had a natural tendency to become: at once refined and profound and remote from the crude realities of urban life.

But the most immediately influential statement establishing the ethos of an educated and cultured élite dominating the whole field of learning and society was Matthew Arnold's *Culture and Anarchy*. Arnold's influence was wide; he was, after all, both an academic and, for most of his career, an Inspector of Schools. That book, as he later remarked, was one of the only books to have become a classic in the lifetime of its author. Arnold found words to give his readers an instant recognition of the intellectual issues of their time. Central to the argument was the fundamental assumption which gives the title to the book. Anarchy was the world of industry and machines and therefore of dehumanisation; culture was the corrective, the answer to it; and the signs of culture were sweetness and light. For culture 'does not try to teach down to the level of inferior classes; it does not try to win them for this or that sect of its own, with ready-made judgements and watchwords. It seeks to do away with classes, to make the best that has been thought and known in the world current everywhere; to make all men live in an atmosphere of sweetness and light, where they may use ideas, as it uses them itself, freely – nourished and not bounded by them'.

With one intellectual leap, Arnold established the ethos of the middle classes and did so in the same decade as Forster's Education Act. It was of course a help in becoming a man of culture if you had a reasonable income already or earned one on the side; but what was clear was that the act of making, a deep involvement with design and technology, could not be a route to culture. The great divide between enlightenment and work was now designated and preserved.

It would be many years, if ever, before the gulf could be bridged between education and work.

These three intellectual expositors, even the many people influenced by them, could not however have established such a complete and lasting outfit of social and educational values if their work had not been reinforced by a conscious or unconscious acceptance of a profound philosophical system. What underlay that intellectual movement was the thought of Plato, and specifically the revival of his thought in the nineteenth century.

It is difficult to exaggerate the importance of this intellectual substratum. It affected in the most fundamental way the entire educational world. And it still does. For the profound attraction of Plato's thought was to offer the intellectual an escape from the mundane world of everyday work and living. Reality was not in that world; reality was in the world of Forms or Ideas, to which the everyday world was a more or less successful approximation. What a wonderful piece of sleight of mind, turning things upside down and finding the most respectable philosophical justification for the privileged world of leisure, discussion and speculation – a pure world of clear and perfect unities not to be found in the imperfect, flawed and confused world of industry and work.

Plato is the ultimate authority for the nineteenth- and twentieth-century concept or idea of a liberal education. What he was not responsible for was that it became a stranglehold upon the whole system. It did so because it neatly fitted the hierarchical character of British society. A liberal education became the peak to which an education should aspire. The ordinary mind dealt with things; the educated mind dealt with ideas. And that had a profound effect upon the most influential institutions.

There seem to be periods in the life of all institutions when their leaders turn in upon themselves and concentrate upon their own self-improvement and self-preservation rather than the service they do to the outside world. Society may now and again hammer upon the door and shout for them to come out and lend a hand in the street; usually there is no answer. Withdrawal from everyday affairs is a constant temptation in the academic world, usually in the universities, today possibly in the former polytechnics; everyday realities are so much less simple than the contemplation of eternal truths. And where better to contemplate them than in the universities, first the ancient colleges of Oxford and Cambridge, then in the provincial universities, founded as colleges for practical training and quickly celebrating their admission into the higher world of learning.

Increasingly, with every year, through the nineteenth and twentieth centuries, the universities and the essential university ethos came to dominate the whole of education. They were the peak, they set the standard, they were a magic world to which the fortunate might one day be admitted. And to make sure of this and fill a gap that might have remained in the circle of education, the Government took a decision in 1917 that was to have the most permanent and drastic effect upon the fortunes of the country.

In that year the Government, in an attempt to rationalise and give some order to the chaos of school-leaving examinations, decreed that the universities would be responsible for conducting those examinations. The system was now complete. For, although it was emphasised by the Board of Education that it should be 'a cardinal principle that the examinations should follow a curriculum and not determine it', in practice the very opposite happened. The examinations were supposed to be school-leaving examinations; they inevitably became qualifying examinations for entry to the universities.

And that had a profound effect upon the whole orientation of studies and teaching. It made entry to the universities the highest aspiration for teachers and pupils, and thus had a profound bearing upon the subjects which would be taught, their nature and scope and the character of the educational experience of the pupils. For it followed from that simple decision that the ethos of the university should become fundamental to the whole of education and training.

And what did the universities deal in? Not training for a job, not developing skills in design and making, not encouraging action; they dealt in learning, grouped into subjects and disciplines and neatly compartmented according to the subject rather than the needs of people or society.

So education became the assembly of subjects and then, at the higher level, disciplines. They, like Platonic forms, had their own essence and boundaries; they were to be handed on, or such parts of them as seemed reasonable to communicate. And what kept them in good shape was more and more study of them, becoming more specialised with every year and eventually, under the influence of Germany and America, rceiving the delectable accolade of research. The academic factory was now in business, sufficient unto itself; research, including literary research about matters so uninteresting that no one was likely to want to do it again, became the aim of the learned and teaching a poor second, not indeed what the professors were there to do. Among that research a small proportion was of the utmost significance for the future of the world. But for the most part, the material poured in and out, weighing down the library floor, becoming sooner or later itself the stuff for more research and more papers. That tradition – and especially the conventional acceptance of what Whitehead called 'inert knowledge' – is so general and established that it still inspires and underlies almost all educational thinking.

To take one relatively recent example, there was issued in 1977 a discusson initiated by the then Prime Minister, James Callaghan, known as the Great Debate and brought together as a Green Paper under the title *Education in Schools: A Consultative Document.* Shirley Williams, the Secretary of State for Education, hosted public meetings throughout the country.

As a well-written summary of a mass of debate by some of the best people in education, it is a document remarkable for its conventionality and its complacency. It is, of course, oriented towards educational administration and politics rather than teaching. But what is particularly fascinating is the list of aims of the schools which 'the majority of people would probably agree with'. Out of eight wordy aims, only one contains – in a phrase tacked on the end, 'giving them the ability ... to apply themselves to tasks' – a hint that it might be good for children to learn to *do* something. There is a reference to engaging in work in primary schools as part of the 'child-centred' approach; but generally education is seen to need more standard assessment and an agreed secondary curriculum for all pupils.

And what that education really consists of is information, critical discussion and appreciation of the mixed economy, the political system and the wealth creating parts of industry. There was no reference to working as part of a team. Supporting it all is the substratum of conventional, accepted values. The gifted will go on to academic studies; the less gifted will turn their attention to careers and the world of work, presumably earning enough to keep the gifted in study. There is no hint that it might be good for the gifted to enter work at the sharp end, and not even a suspicion that there might be something to be said for learning to do things, to make things, to invent, to wonder, to discover the fascination of nature and things and the fantastic possibilities in doing and making. Even though it is familiar knowledge that if you want to cultivate a habit or a skill or an attitude, you must start it early, it seems to have been forgotten that the conventional kind of schooling might be re-examined, to ask at least if there might be a more real and fundamental way of learning to take part in an urban industrial society than just to add to the curriculum a few classes of appreciation.

And yet, for many years, there has been no shortage of people commenting on the dangers inherent in our attitudes and warning us of what might happen – warnings that now seem only too perceptive of the reality that would overtake us. Over 100 years ago, in 1869, Herbert Spencer wrote:

That which our school courses leave almost entirely out, we thus find to be what most nearly concerns the business of life. Our industries would cease, were it not for the information which men acquire, as best they may, after their education is said to be finished. The vital knowledge – that by which we have grown as a nation to what we are, and which now underlies our whole existence – is a knowledge that has got itself taught in nooks and corners, while the ordained agencies for teaching have been mumbling little else but dead formulae.

The knowledge that got itself taught in nooks and corners was the start of the ability to control the physical world. And if it had to do with control, it must have something to do with technology. But what in a serious educational argument, did we mean by technology?

Technology is not 'applied science'. A myth has grown up in recent years that applied science and technology are the same. It is probably the result of the status system I have already described: rubbing shoulders with science would give technology a little more respectability in the academic world. Technology is not applied science and never was for the simple reason that it started differently.

The origins of technology lie in the solving of practical problems. In that sense the great engineers – Telford and Stephenson, Brunel and Brindley, like the leading engineers of today, whose work includes some of the greatest wonders of our time – were practical men with a massive dose of common sense, enormous energy and the ability to devise ingenious solutions to definable problems. Their work arose initially not from the application of scientific theories and principles to a practical situation, but the opposite. It was the solution to problems that provided the material from which to deduce a scientific principle.

That was generally true of the ancient world as of that of primitive man, the toolmaker. *Technique precedes science.* But it was with the development of science that technique was able to progress; and that was a nineteenth-century phenomenon. As inventions were built upon the work of

scientists and scientific principles were deduced from technological inventions, the two activities increasingly over-
lapped and their boundaries became less sharply defined.
But essentially technology is an activity in its own right,
with its own objectives and skills. Technology, to quote
Robert M. Pirsig's bestseller *Zen and the Art of Motorcycle
Maintenance*:

> is simply the making of things and the making of things
> can't, by its own nature be ugly or there would be no
> possibility for beauty in the arts, which also include the
> making of things. Actually a root word for technology,
> *techne*, originally meant 'art'. The ancient Greeks never
> separated art from manufacture in their minds, and so
> never developed separate words for them.

Techne means art and craft; *logos* means word or speech.
To the Greeks technology, had they used the formulation,
would have meant a discourse upon the arts, pure and
applied. For us it has come mainly to mean, from the
seventeenth century onwards, the applied arts and more
specifically the means and processes, the tools and
machines, which are the means to an end – the product. A
typically modern view, in the latest edition of the *Encyclopedia Britannica*, is that 'technology is the means or activity
by which man seeks to change or manipulate his environment'. The earlier versions are more helpful because they
imply something of the scope of the activity, the universality
of its significance, and its essentially creative nature. For me
it is a systematic approach to the practical arts. And that
has wide ramifications. Wider even than Gordon Childe's
account in Singer's *History of Technology*; that technology
'should mean the study of those activities, directed to the
satisfaction of human needs, which produce alterations in
the material world'.

In particular I want to emphasise, because even technolo-
gists often fail to recognise it, that technology requires
creativity. Common sense tells us that, in any case. To put

171

it in more current terminology, technology includes design. In the wide and comprehensive way in which I am discussing it, technology can be described as *creative ingenuity*. The phrase is not unusual. But it was used to considerable effect in the late 1970s in articles in *The Times Higher Education Supplement* and other journals in which the author, Michael Fores, made some provocative and persuasive points.

In Mr Fores' view, the real cultural divide of our day is not that between the well-known 'two cultures' of C. P. Snow, but one between *all* the useful arts and professions on the one hand, and *all* areas of scholarship, including science and the fine arts, on the other – between, in one formulation, technology and the rest. Mankind, he considered, can be more realistically divided into *homo sapiens*, concerned with reflection and ultimately with wisdom, and *homo faber*, whose concern is with making and using tools to extend his direct and personal powers. *Homo faber* is creative, not because of some instant vision of the kind often attributed to artists (though my own background in art and design does not tell me of many such moments of instant genius) but because of long periods of work, struggling with the subject matter and making useful artefacts as a result of creative activity. Man the maker is the creator of products.

Whatever field one looks at in the world of contemporary technology, the fact is, in Mr Fores' words, that 'in every case of major technical advance, the most crucial factors have been the pioneer's conception of design and manufacture, of basic need and utility, coupled with his ability to worry his way through to his goal'. In other words, the root of technology is creative ingenuity. Thus technology at its simplest (and I suspect at its most complicated) is concerned with solving other people's problems. It requires the clear statement of the problem, the consideration of alternatives and the elimination of the inappropriate, the following of a regular procedure, and some kind of quantitative assessment.

That is not to say that it is concerned *only* with the quantitative, the measurable, the calculable. Technology, as something involving innovation and change – creative ingenuity – demands an exercise of the imagination as much as of the intellect (if the two can be considered separately). There is no doubt, in the field of engineering, of the use of intuition as well as calculation – that is to say, not a wild emotional grasping at straws, but the use of a direct way of grasping the solution to a problem, not usually in one leap but as part of a continuing experience.

Technical education, in Whitehead's words, 'is creative experience while you think, experience which realises your thought, experience which teaches you to co-ordinate act and thought, experience leading you to associate thought with foresight and foresight with achievement. Technical education gives theory, and a shrewd insight as to where theory fails'. Here is a clear and simple statement of the process at the most ordinary level – in the field of motor cycle maintenance – from Pirsig's *Zen and the Art of Motorcycle Maintenance*:

If you have to choose among an infinite number of ways to put it together then the relation of the machine to you, and the relation of the machine and you to the rest of the world, has to be considered, because the selection from among many choices, the *art* of the work is just as dependent upon your own mind and spirit as it is upon the material of the machine. That's why you need peace of mind ... Sometime look at a novice workman or a bad workman and compare his expression with that of a craftsman whose work you know is excellent and you will know the difference. The craftsman isn't following a single line of instruction. He's making decisions as he goes along. For that reason, he'll be absorbed and attentive to what he's doing even though he doesn't deliberately contrive this. His motions and the machine are in a kind of harmony. He isn't following any set of written instructions because the nature of the material at hand determines his thoughts and motions, which simultaneously change the nature of the material at hand. The material and his thoughts are changing together in a progression of changes until his mind's at rest at the same time's the material's right. 'Sounds like art,' the instructor says. 'Well it is *art*,' I say. 'This divorce of art from technology is completely unnatural. It's just that it's gone on so long you have to be an archaeologist to find out where the two separated.

This expresses colourfully the problems I began to recognise in defining the fundamental unity of a polytechnic. And it was echoed in a serious study entitled *Engineering: Our Future*, the report of the Committee of Inquiry into the engineering profession chaired by Sir Montague Finniston in 1980. In referring to the tradition in the German *Technische Hochschule* and French *Grandes Écoles*, based firmly upon the philosophy and concept of *Technik*, the synthesis and practical application of knowledge rather than of scientific scholarship, the Report insisted that (my emphasis added)

This view of engineering science as an offshoot or application of science is held to have underlain many of the current criticisms of engineering formation in Britain today; in particular, engineering courses constructed on the basis of teaching first the underlying scientific analysis and theory and then the potential applications of it, build into engineering formation a dichotomy between 'theory' and 'practice'. This dichotomy does not arise in courses based upon the philosophy of 'Technik' which places everything taught firmly in the context of economic purpose. Theoretical teaching is from early on linked to its potential usefulness within the overall theme of an engineering system, be it mechanical, electrical or process. The final years of 'German model' and French engineering courses are then concentrated upon specialised projects designed to focus and bring together what had been learnt about various aspects of a particular system. The debate which has continually dogged engineering teachers over the appropriate balance in engineering formation between theory and practice is a non-issue within the continental mode of engineering teaching. This deficiency to a large extent reflects the relatively restricted and narrow British conception of engineering as a branch of applied science, which militates against an effective marriage between theory and application.

I became convinced that the polytechnic for which I was responsible, and which I had founded, ought to be involved in the pursuit of a much clearer understanding of its potential contribution to higher education. I was not alone. Many of us, not only in the polytechnic, wrote and lectured on the subject. We felt strongly about the real needs of higher – and indeed all – education.

In 1977 the head of the small business section of the London Business School, Peter Gorb, invited about twenty of us who had been writing on the subject for *The Times Higher Education Supplement* to meet at the School in London to discuss the need. Using the ditinction drawn by Michael Fores between *homo sapiens* and *homo faber*, he assembled us under the title *Homo Faber*. The meeting included both Michael Fores and Sir Toby Weaver. After protracted discussion and general agreement, we decided that Homo Faber might not be the correct title and adopted one based on a paper by Weaver and renamed ourselves *Education for Capability*.

Our manifesto, which was soon composed, read:

There is a serious imbalance in Britain today in the full process which is described by the two words 'education' and 'training'. The idea of the 'educated person' is that of a scholarly individual who has been neither educated nor trained to exercise useful skills; who is able to understand but not to act. Young people in secondary or higher education increasingly specialize, and do so too often in ways which mean that they are taught to practise only the skills of scholarship and science. They acquire knowledge of particular subjects, but are not equipped to use knowledge in ways which are relevant to the world outside the education system.

This imbalance is harmful to individuals, to industry and to society. A well-balanced education should, of course, embrace analysis and the acquisition of knowledge. But it must also include the exercise of creative skills, the competence to undertake the complete tasks and the ability to cope with everyday life; and also doing all these things in co-operation with others.

There exists in its own right a culture which is concerned with doing, making and organising and the creative arts. This culture emphasises the day to day management of affairs, the formulation and solution of problems and the design, manufacture and marketing of goods and services.

Educators should spend more time preparing people in this way for a life outside the education system. The country would benefit significantly in economic terms from what is here described as 'Education for Capability'.

But I was still searching for a real meaning for the polytechnic, for a basic set of principles that would lie behind everything we did or developed. Within the polytechnic I made it clear that I would not approve any proposed course that did not have in principle a job at the end. We were or ought to be the apostles of doing and making and that must be the meaning of 'polytechnic': many arts and many skills.

We ought to be able to teach appropriately. For the world of human endeavour, what kind of mind, what abilities are needed? My argument was as follows. To start with, it is necessary to put things in the right order. We would all agree that literacy and numeracy are crucial in our society. But it is easy to think of them as ends in themselves. They

176

are not ends but means to something else – to understanding and to action. They are necessary but not sufficient. We need at least a third means or ability which has a direct bearing upon the modern world. This must have to do with visual awareness or acuity – the ability to perceive and understand in three dimensions. It is necessary for the understanding of many subjects, like advanced mathematics; it is essential for producion work, for design of all kinds. And design is the one underrated activity which is central to every single technological and environmental development happening in front of our eyes. It is not art in the sense of aesthetics; it is not whimsy; it is not an expression of conventional taste; it is the thinking out of objects and processes which shape our lives. And whether or not people are trained specifically in design, design is being carried out all the time.

If to these activities – literacy, numeracy and spatial awareness – we add manual skill, the world of learning takes on a different shape. For manual skill as I understand it is not just a description of a physical event but of an activity which involves the mind and body and also requires will-power. Skills, if applied at the level which our advanced society demands, cannot be discussed in terms of the traditional dualism of mind and body. There is much more involved. It must include decision making and the carrying out of decisions, whether our own or those of others. Addressing a conference on higher education in Newcastle in 1976 (*'Higher education: for what and for whom?'*), Sir Toby Weaver put it this way:

I am thinking of a person's general capacity to manage his own life, to cope with his environment, to profit from experience, to master what used to be called the art of living, to reach sensible decisions and act on them. To call this quality gumption or *nous* is to incur the charge of vulgarity; to call it wisdom verges on the highfaluting; to call it lifemanship lacks seriousness. May I settle for CAPABILITY as the nearest I can get to describing the ability to apply one's stock of knowledge and manifold of skills, as Bacon put it, for the benefit and use of man.

Here was the explanation of *Capability*. It followed that the sources of material for our education, the generators of our total experience, could not simply be words and certainly not just books. They are, so to speak, 'out there'. In that sense, the centre of a useful education is not really the library. The library is an essential tool, but there are many others. They include fact, lives, other people – in short, real life.

Real life is never as neat as the scholar's summary in his book. In real life one can never get all the information, and much of what he gets is contradictory. This is why simple answers to complex questions are not very educational. The point is that young people must be educated to look for data outside books so that they will be better able to handle the world outside academia. The professors in our universities too often try to make students into carbon copies of themselves.

This remark came in a thought-provoking paper by the Director of the East-West Center at Honolulu, Mr Everett Kleinjans. For him, in the new situation we are trying to develop, the student must begin to look for data in the reality of society and not just in his Professor's lectures, the library or the laboratory. In fact, the street, the town, the field become his primary sources. He learns to deal with the knowledge of everyday life. His task is to figure out how to make order out of complexity or chaos. And that involves a new look at the nature of knowledge. In that paper, Kleinjans quoted Drucker (*The Age of Discontinuity*, 1969): 'For the intellectual knowledge is what is in a book. But as long as it is in the book, it is only "information" if not mere "data". Only when a man applies the information to do something does it become knowledge. Knowledge, like elec-

178

tricity or money, is a form of energy that exists only when doing work.'

It must be the case that such knowledge cannot be acquired in isolation or privacy; it requires cooperation. It may be the case that an in-depth study can be carried out in isolation. However, the *application* of that study undoubtedly demands collaboration – the joint pursuit of what Whitehead called 'the art of the utilisation of knowledge'.

It remained my ambition to make Leeds Polytechnic the finest teaching organisation in Europe. We did our best to provide appropriate training. University teachers were never trained; it was assumed that mastery of a subject was all that was necessary and that students would pick up fragments of learning dropped by the lecturer. The standard of teaching in any university I knew was generally deplorable. In contrast we introduced new members of staff to what we called not teacher training but 'Polytechnic Resources for Learning'. And we developed sequences of learning that were psychologically more appropriate than the conventional methods. For example, university teachers and college of education teachers usually start a course with general principles, look at them in more detail and then discuss how they could be applied. Our view was that, psychologically, the correct sequence was different: it was to look at a problem in detail, find out how to solve it and then produce generalisations. The principle I announced many times was this: the task of a polytechnic teacher is to teach a subject so well and train the students so effectively that they can abstract for themselves general principles which will then be applicable in a situation unforeseen.

As I finish writing and reading these chapters and appendix, I recognise that in many ways I have acted as a catalyst in making changes in the system of higher and further education. And I ask myself whether that continual effort has in fact helped the scene to change. It is clear that student demand is persuading many universities to modify their studies. It has indeed been argued that many universities have been converted into polytechnics.